Content

Module 1 1
Module 2 5
Module 3 10
Module 4 14
Module 5 18
Module 6 24
Module 7 33
Module 8 38
Module 9 41
Module 10 45
Module 11 49
Module 12 52
Module 13 60
Module 14 65
Module 15 69
Module 16 74
Module 17 82
Module 18 87
Cutouts 98
Sight Words 202

© 2020 by Accelerate Education
Visit us on the Web at: www.accelerate.education

My name is _____.

1) Follow the model and finger trace A and a, then read the sentence aloud.

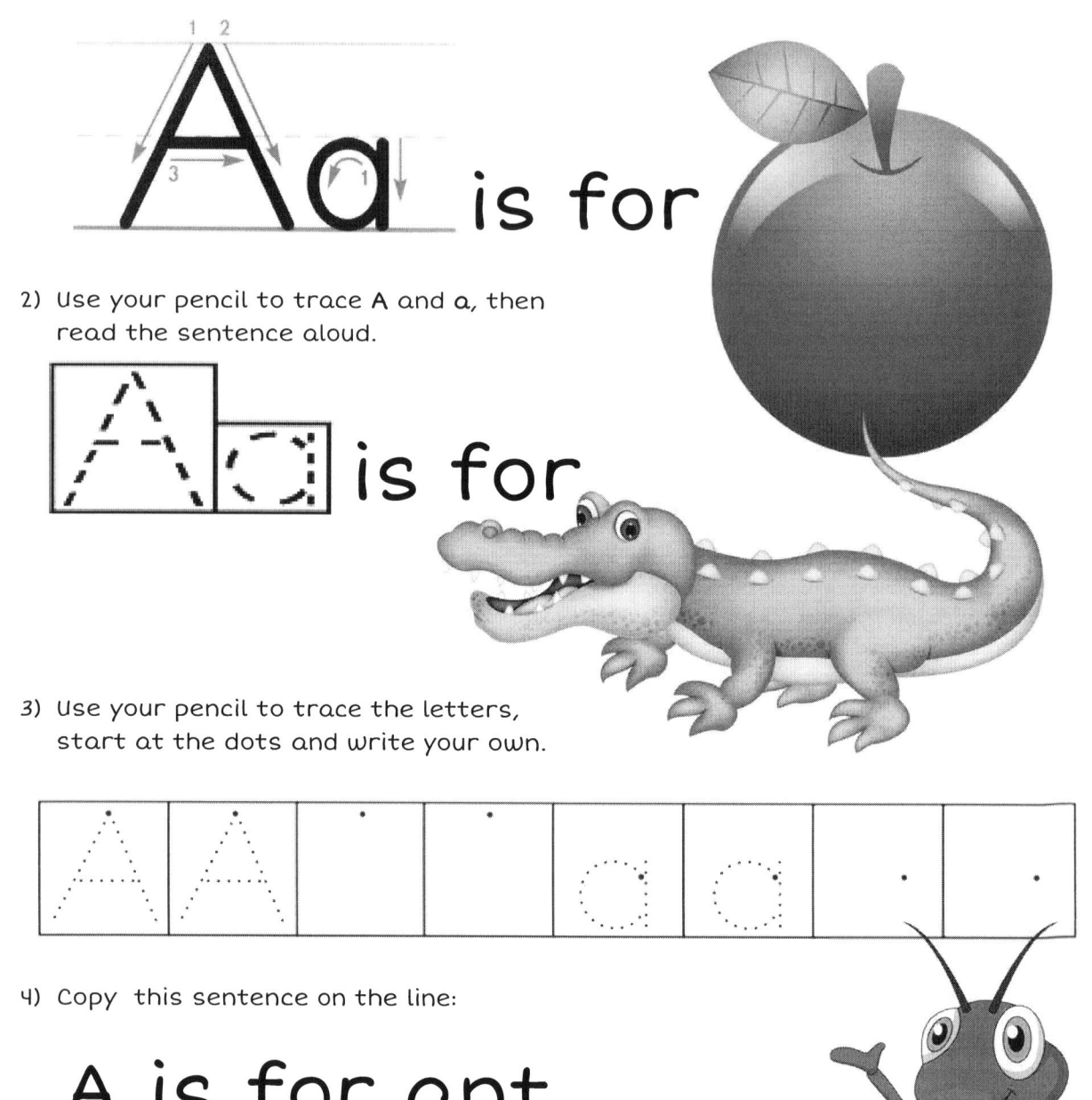

Aa is for

2) Use your pencil to trace A and a, then read the sentence aloud.

Aa is for

3) Use your pencil to trace the letters, start at the dots and write your own.

4) Copy this sentence on the line:

A is for ant.

1　　　　　　　　　　　　　　　　　　　　　　　　　　　　　1.1 - Letter Aa

My name is _____.
Draw a picture of your favorite activity you did this summer.

1.4 - Letter Aa

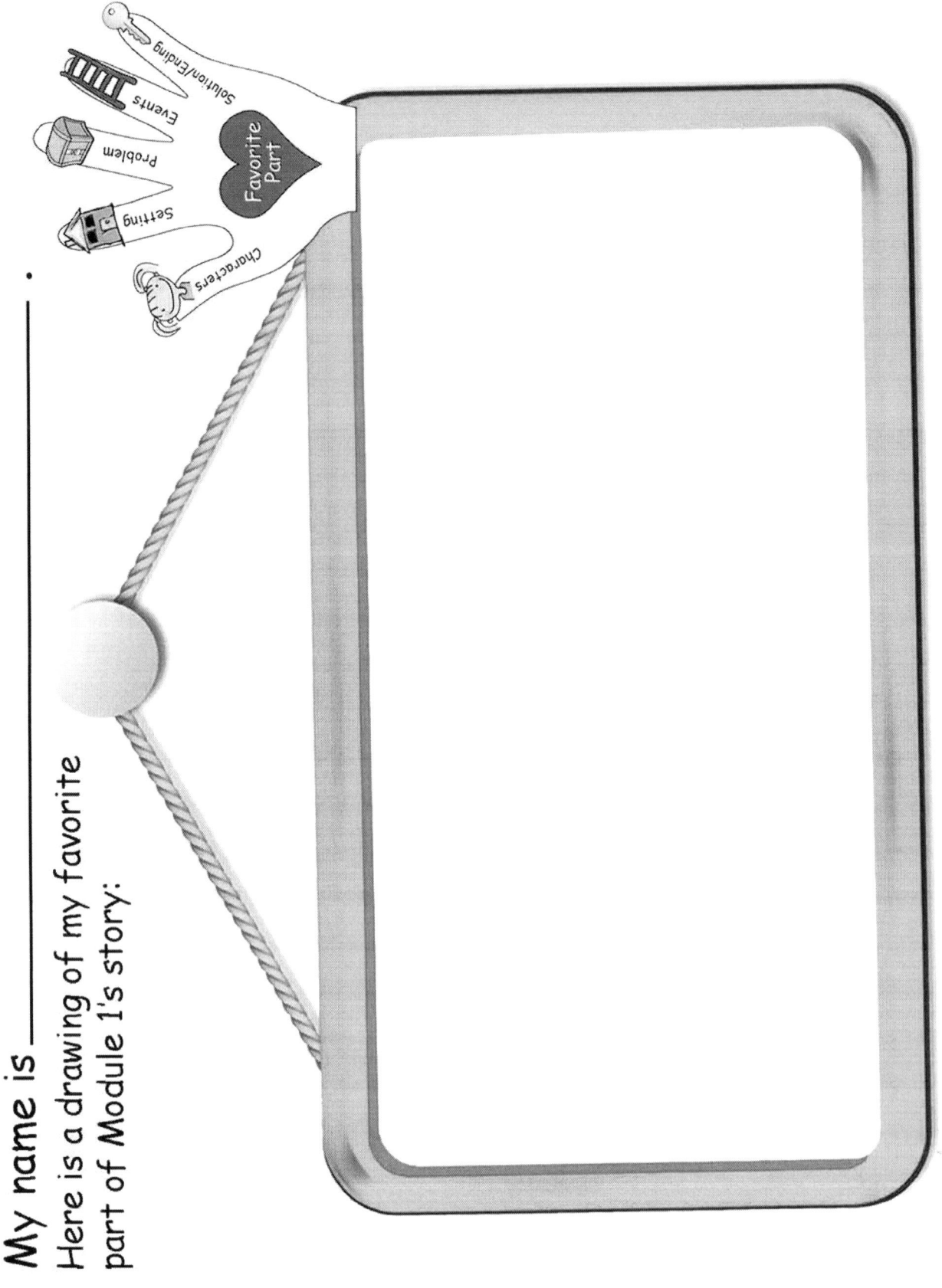

My name is _____.

Here is a drawing of my favorite part of Module 1's story:

My name is _____.

Wrap it up!

1) Fill in the blank with a word that starts with a letter from the bank. Write the sentence on the lines.
2) Draw a picture for your sentence in the box.
3) Underline your sight words with a yellow line.

A Word Bank:
ax
ant
apple

I see a big a_____.

1.5 - Letter Aa

My name is _____ .

1) Follow the model and finger trace **B** and **b**, then read the sentence aloud.

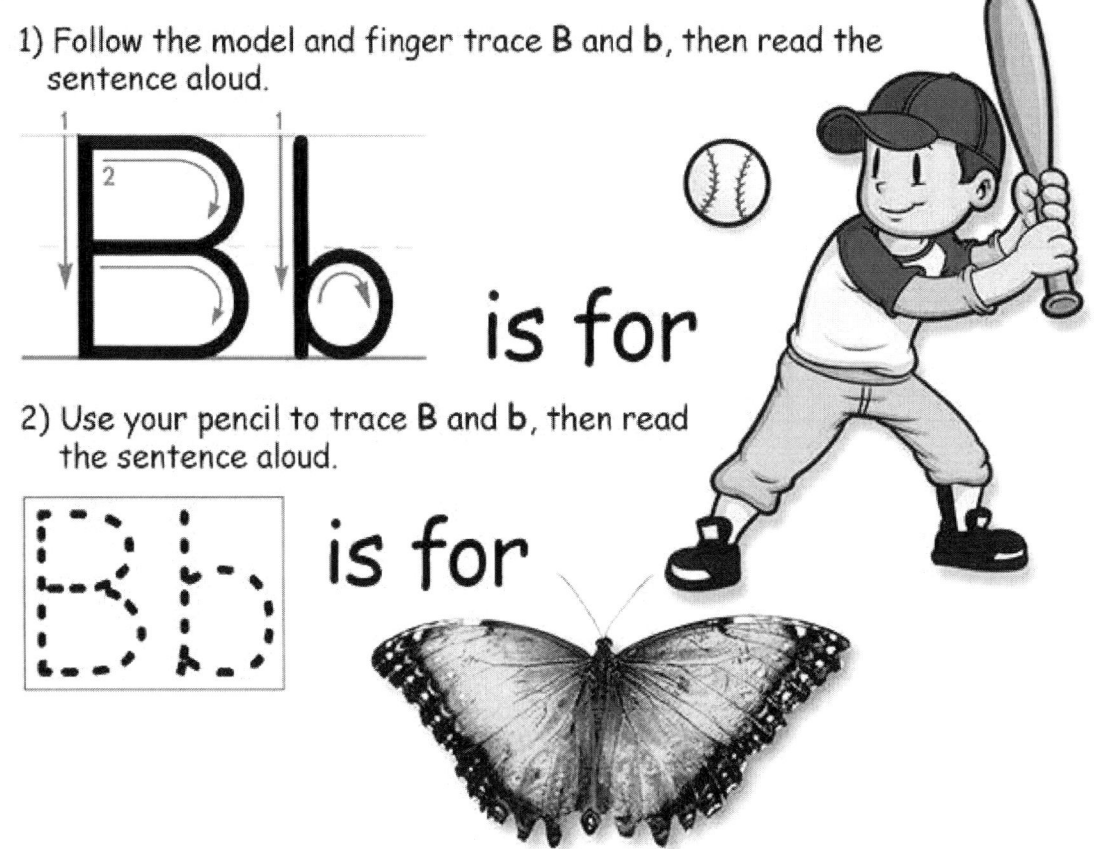

Bb is for

2) Use your pencil to trace **B** and **b**, then read the sentence aloud.

Bb is for

3) Use your pencil to trace the letters in the boxes then start at the dots and write your own.

4) Copy this sentence on the line below:

B is for bear.

My name is _____.

It's Rhyme Time!

Draw a picture of something that rhymes with the **b** word in the box to the right.

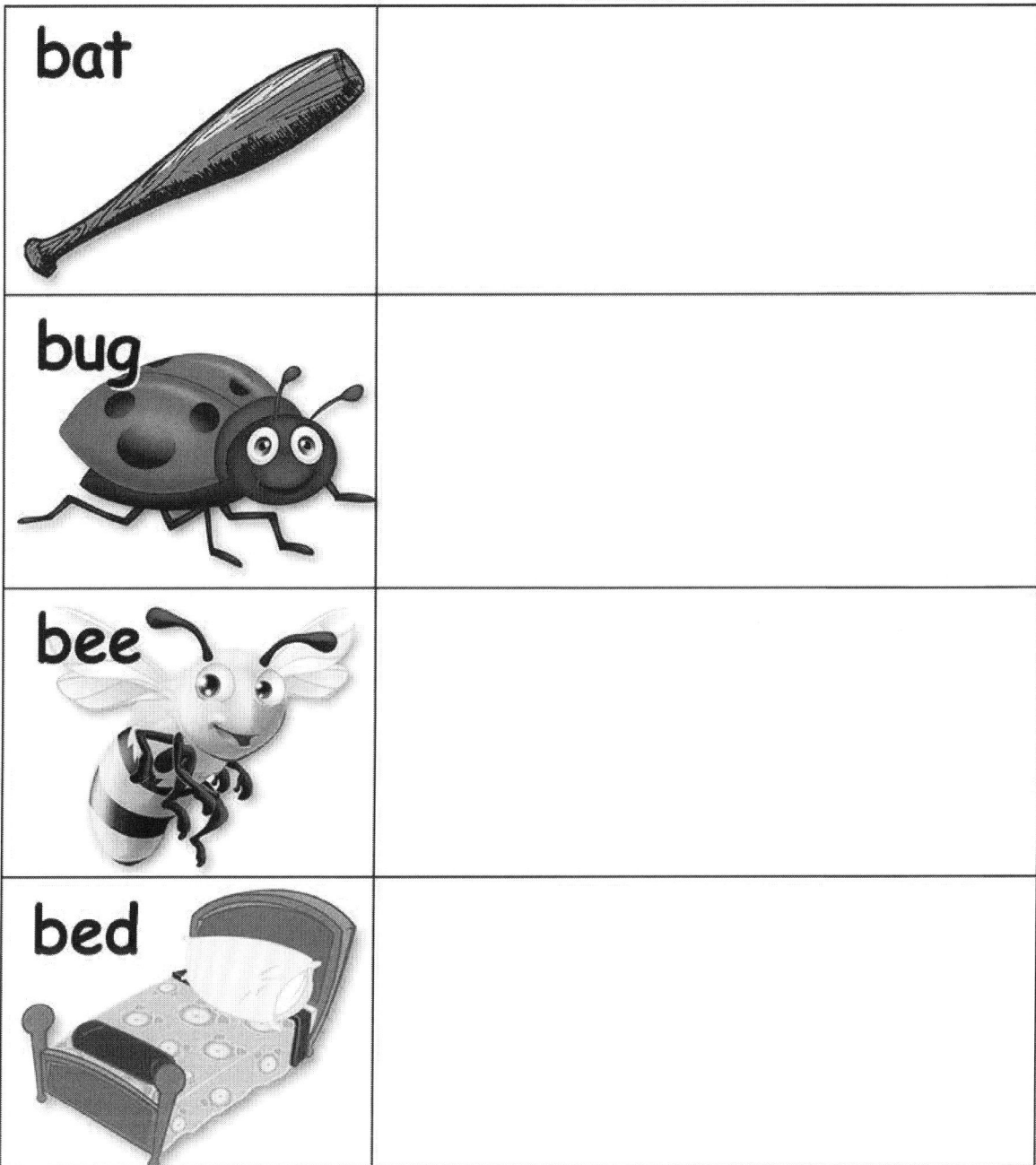

2.2 - Letter Bb

My name is _____.

Draw a picture of how you felt after your favorite summer activity from Module 1.

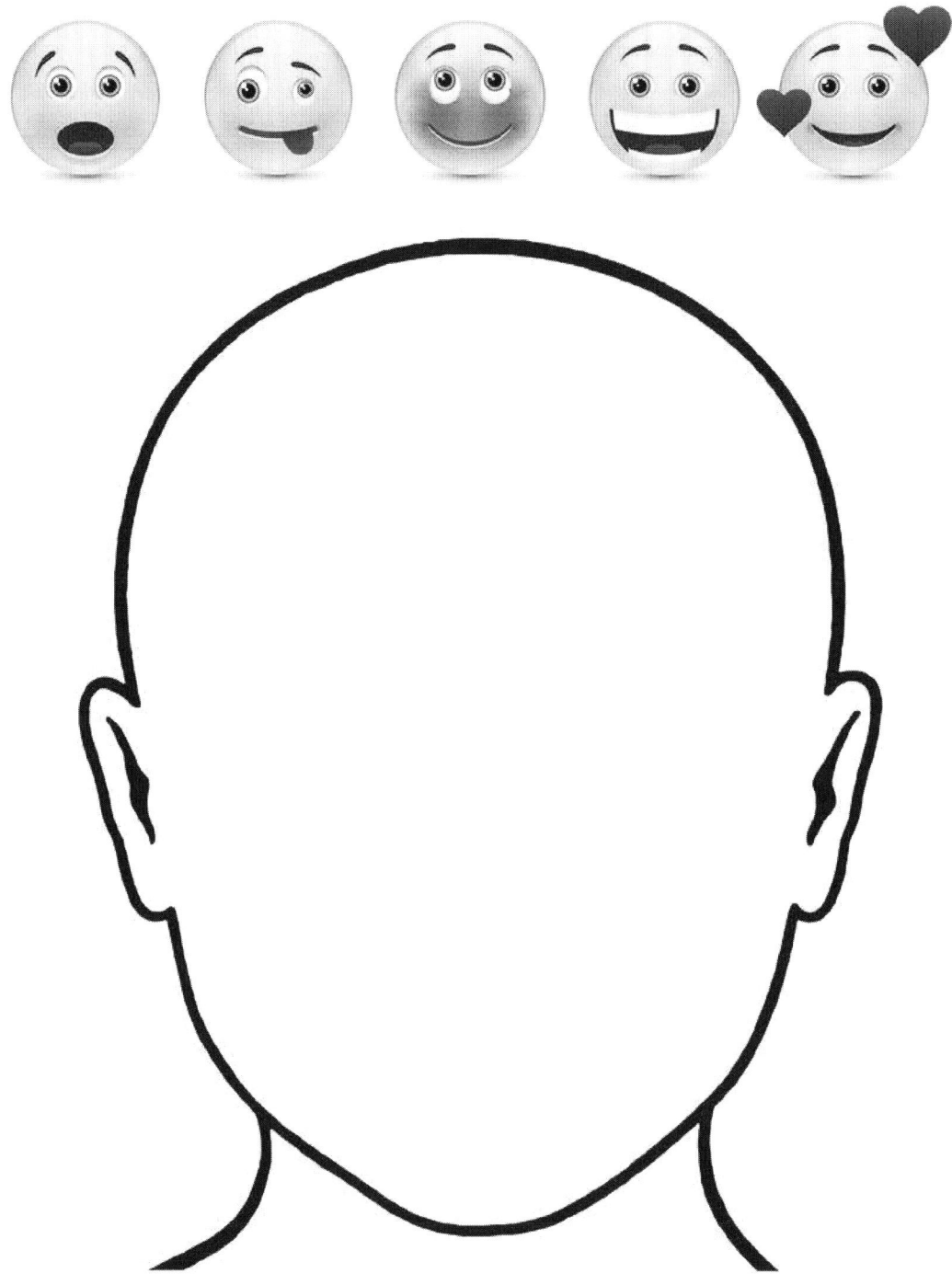

7   2.4 - Letter Bb

My name is _____.
Draw the setting to Module 2's story.

My name is _____.

Wrap it up!

1) Fill in the blank with a B word from the bank.
2) Write the sentence on the lines.
3) Draw a picture for your sentence in the box.
4) Underline your sight words with a yellow line.

WORD BANK:
bird
bear
boy
bat

A blue _____ can sing.

2.5 - Letter Bb

My name is _____.

1) Follow the model and finger trace T and t, then read the sentence aloud.

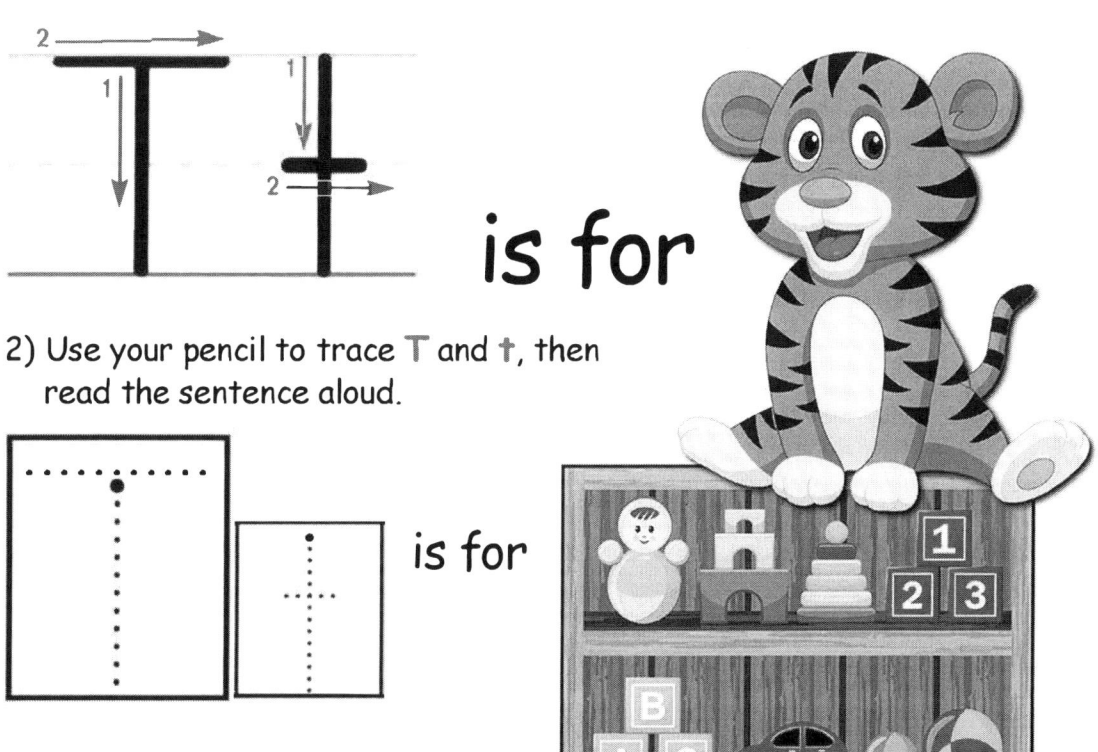

is for

2) Use your pencil to trace T and t, then read the sentence aloud.

is for

3) Use your pencil to trace the letters in the boxes then start at the dots and write your own.

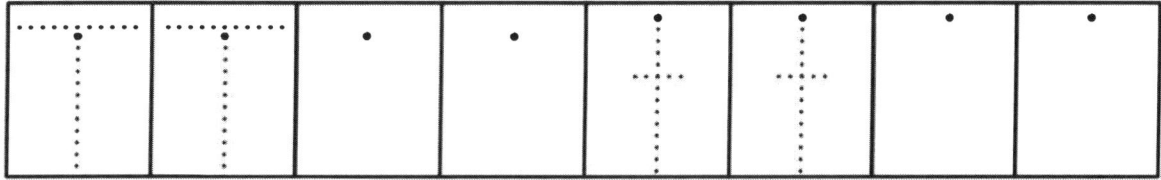

4) Copy this sentence on the line below:

T is for ten.

3.1 - Letter Tt

My name is _____.

Directions: Use elbow macaroni and glue them in the boxes below to make the quotation marks.

Example:

The 🐱 said, " Meow."

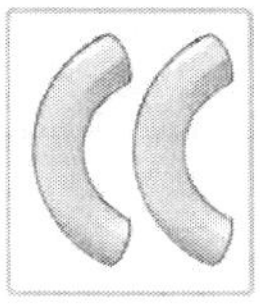

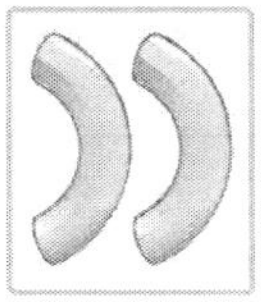

The  🐕 said, ☐ Woof. ☐

The 🐄 said, ☐ Moo. ☐

The 🐖 said, ☐ Oink. ☐

The 🦆 said, ☐ Quack. ☐

3.2 - Letter Tt

3.5 - Letter Tt

My name is _____.

Wrap it up!

1) Fill in the blanks with **T** words from the Word Bank.
2) Write the sentence on the lines.
3) Draw a picture for your sentence in the box.
4) Underline your sight words with a yellow line.

WORD BANK:
turkey   train
tiger   truck
toad   tricycle
tortoise tractor
turtle   trolley

The t_____ said, "I see a big t_____."

13   3.5 - Letter Tt

My name is _____ .

1) Follow the model and finger trace **M** and **m**, then read the sentence aloud.

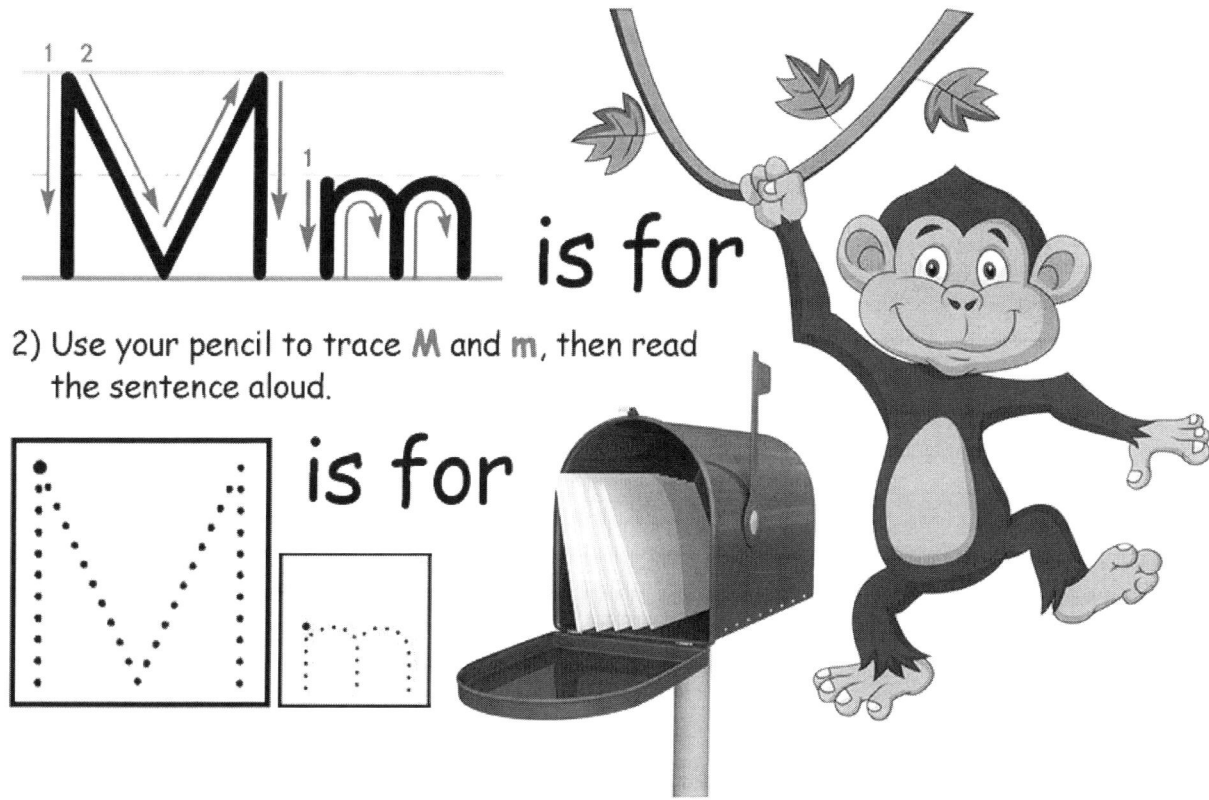

2) Use your pencil to trace **M** and **m**, then read the sentence aloud.

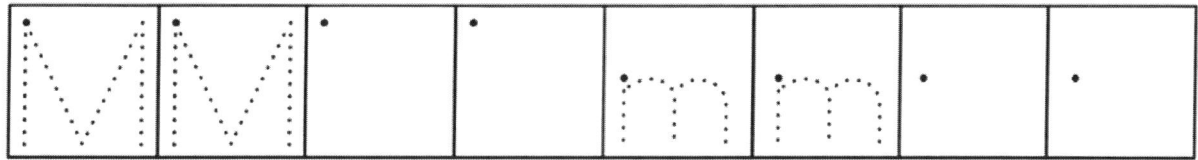

3) Use your pencil to trace the letters in the boxes then start at the dots and write your own.

4) Copy this sentence on the line below:

M is for milk.

4.1 - Letter Mm

My name is _____ .

Trace the verb word and draw a line to match it to the picture. Then act out the verb.

P_ _ _ _ _ _

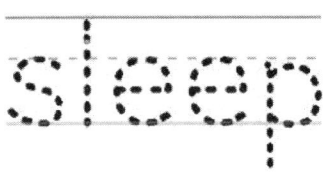

C_ _ _ _ _ _
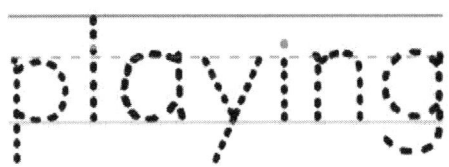

S_ _ _

P_ _ _ _

S_ _ _ _

15   4.2 - Letter Mm

My name is _____.

MAKING CONNECTIONS

When I read this in the story,

It reminds me of …

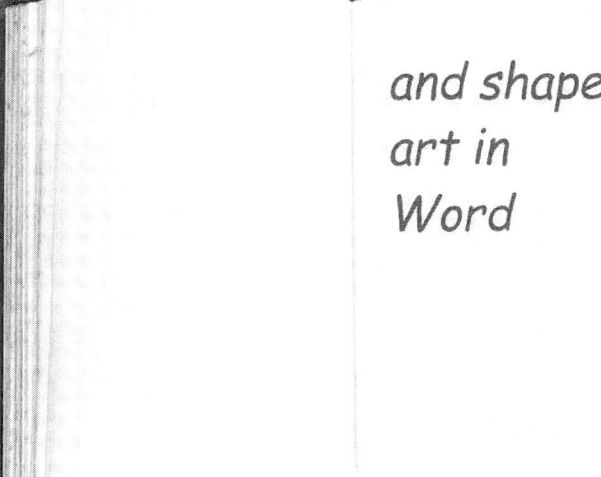

and shape art in Word

Text

to

Self

My name is _____.

Wrap it up!

1) Fill in the blank with an **M** word from the bank.
2) Write the sentence on the lines.
3) Draw a picture for your sentence in the box.
4) Underline your sight words with a yellow line.

WORD BANK:
milk
muffins
meat
melons
mangos

I will go for _____. It is yummy!

4.5 - Letter Mm

My name is _____ .

1) Follow the model and finger trace S and s, then read the sentence aloud.

2) Use your pencil to trace S and s, then read the sentence aloud.

3) Use your pencil to trace the letters in the boxes then start at the dots and write your own.

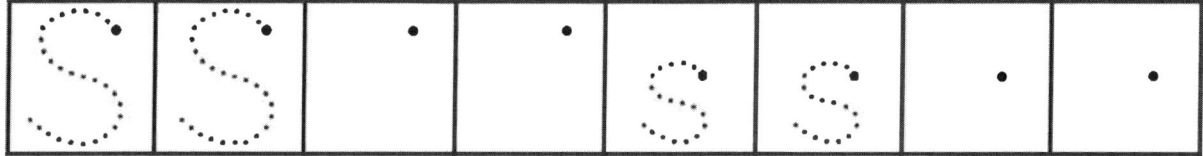

4) Copy this sentence on the line below:

S is for smile.

5.1 - Letter Ss

My name is _____.

Labeling Events

Directions:

Label the events of the story, "Smile!" by ear spelling.

1) Look at the picture of the word you are to label.

2) Say the word out loud and listen to the sounds.

3) Ear spell the word by writing any letters you know for the sounds of the word on the line.

Beginning:

Continue on next page.

Middle:

_____
- - - - -
_____

_____
- - - - -
_____

_____
- - - - -
_____

Continue on next page.

5.4 - Letter Ss

End:

My name is _____.

??? Question Words ???
Who are you?

Book: Module 5's Story from your Reading Chart

Directions:
1) Draw a picture from the story that answers each question word.
2) Label your picture with ear spelling.

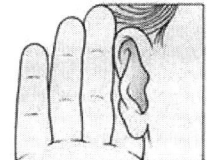

Who	What
When	Where

5.5 - Letter Ss

My name is _____.

Wrap it up!

1) Fill in the blank with an **S** word from the bank.
2) Write the sentence on the lines.
3) Draw a picture for your sentence in the box.
4) Underline your sight words with a yellow line.

WORD BANK:
Snake   Skunk
Swan   Shark
Sheep   Seal
Squirrel

_____, come down here.

My name is _____ .

1) Follow the model and finger trace **N** and **n**, then read the sentence aloud.

2) Use your pencil to trace **N** and **n**, then read the sentence aloud.

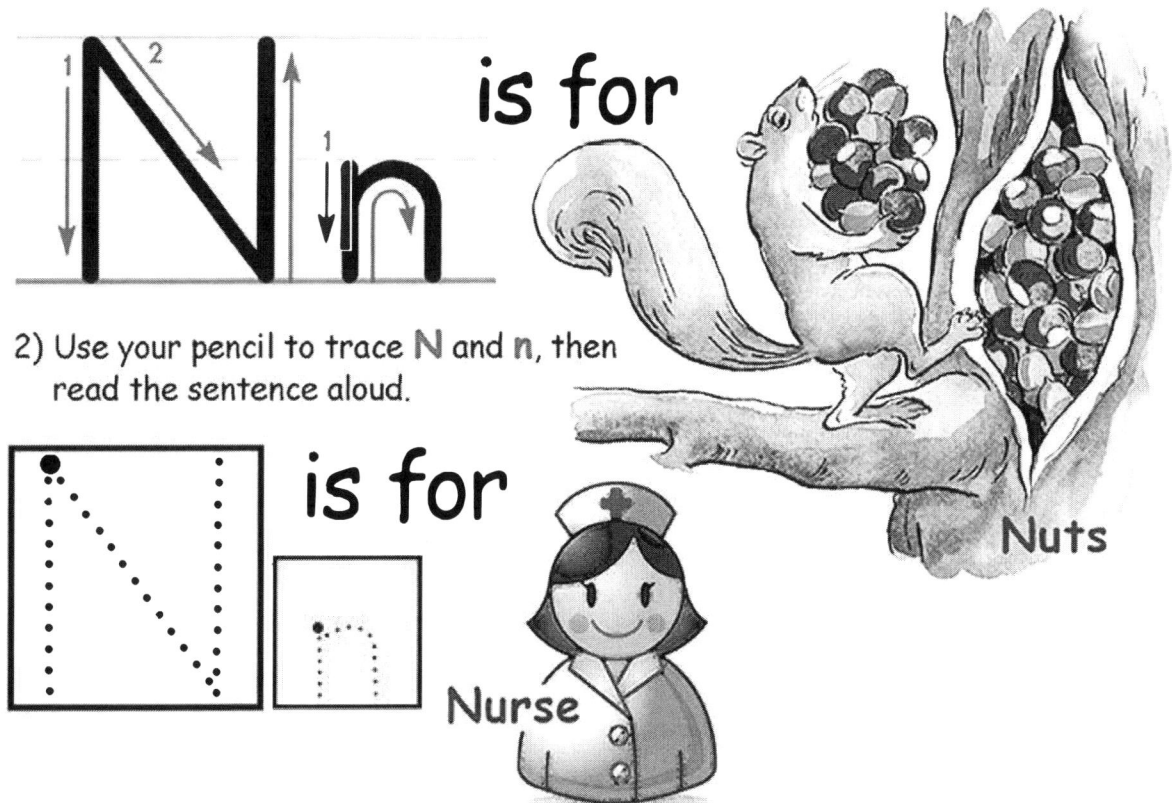

3) Use your pencil to trace the letters in the boxes then start at the dots and write your own.

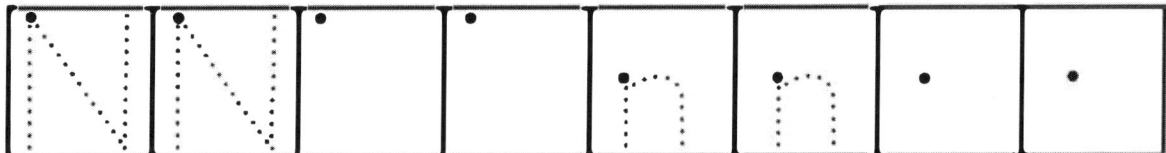

4) Copy this sentence on the line below and read it out loud:

N is for nine.

6.1 - Letter Nn

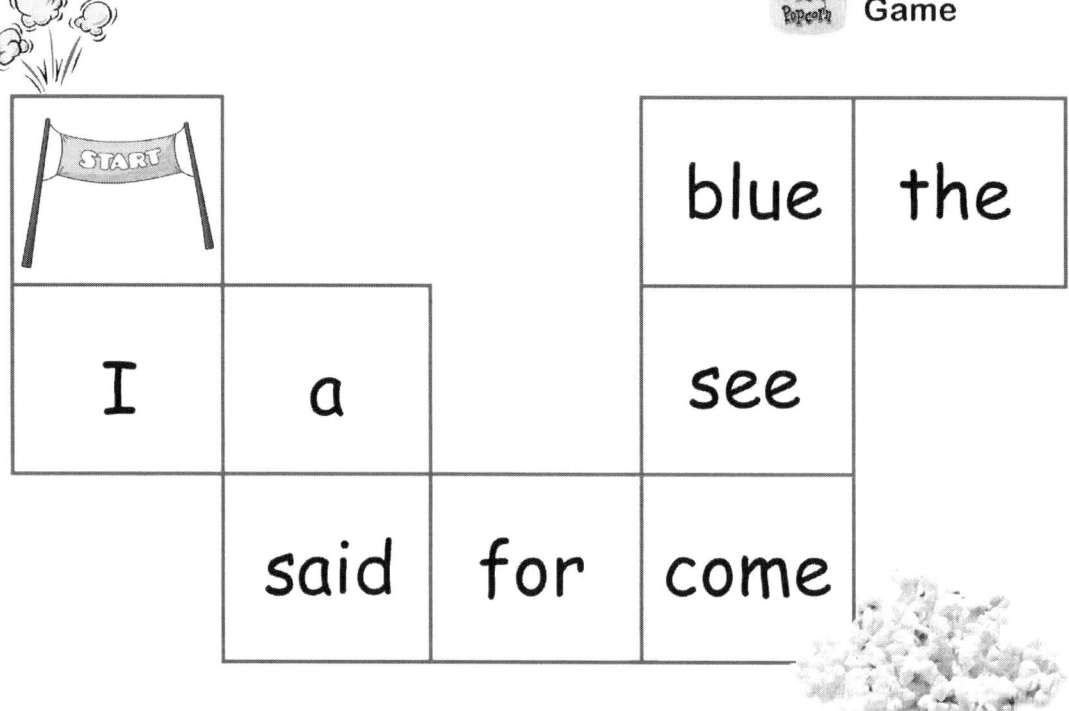

My name is _____ .

Spaghetti and Meatballs Spaces

Spaghetti spaces are small spaces between letters in a word.

Meatball spaces are big spaces between words.

S p a g h e t t i

1) Draw spaghetti lines between the letters to show small spaces with a yellow colored pencil:

s e e   b i g   b l u e   c a n

s a i d   t h e   i n   f o r

i s   g o   c o m e   h e r e

I • like • spaghetti • and • meatballs.

2) Draw a meatball between the words to show the spaces with a brown colored pencil:

I can see a big can.

The blue can is in the box.

 My name is _____.

Write all of these sentences on the lines below.
Then read them out loud.

I can see a blue net.

I said, "The big newt is in the can."

I can go for nachos.

Continue on following page

Come down here!

6.3 - Letter Nn

Writing Web: Favorite Animal

1. Choose your favorite animal as the topic for your writing web.

2. Draw a picture in the middle circle and label it by ear spelling.

3. Think of four details to describe your favorite animal. Draw a picture in each circle and label your pictures with ear spelling.

Example:

Here is an example of a Web on the topic of **cats**. Your web outline is on the next page. Make your own.

Continue on next page.

My name is _____ .

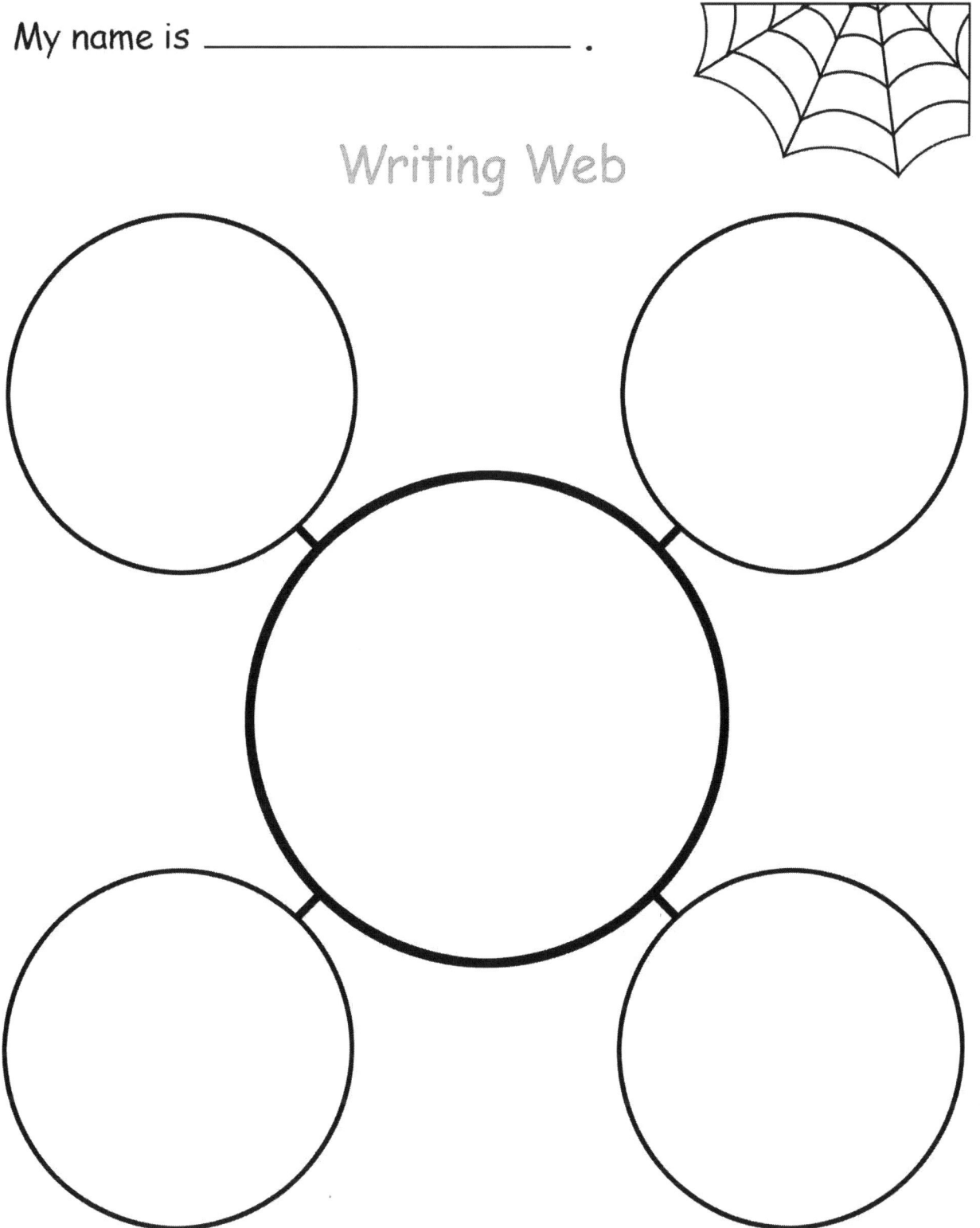

Writing Web

6.4 - Letter Nn

My name is _____ .

Missing Letters
Trace the missing letters:

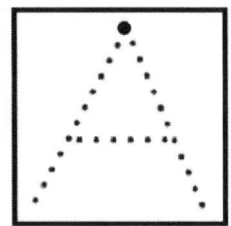 

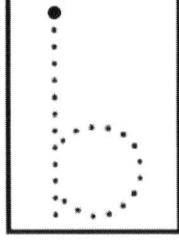ear 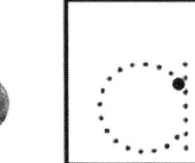nd

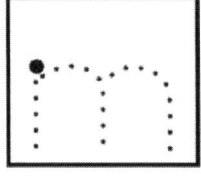onkey 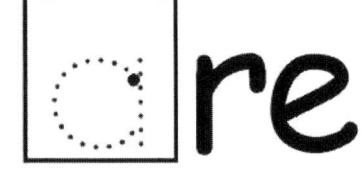re

te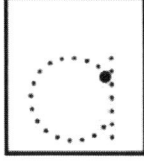i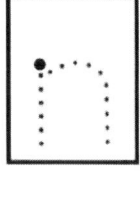g the

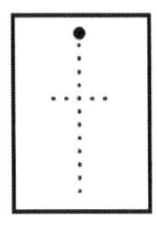iger.

My name is _____ .

Wrap it up!

Write a sentence with these sight words and draw a picture for it. Don't forget the first letter should be capital and you need a period at the end.

My Sight Words

| I | see | big | blue | can | said | the | in |
| for | is | go | come | here | down | a | |

My name is _____ .

1) Follow the model and finger trace **E** and **e**, then read the sentence aloud.

2) Use your pencil to trace **E** and **e**, then read the sentence aloud.

3) Use your pencil to trace the letters in the boxes then start at the dots and write your own.

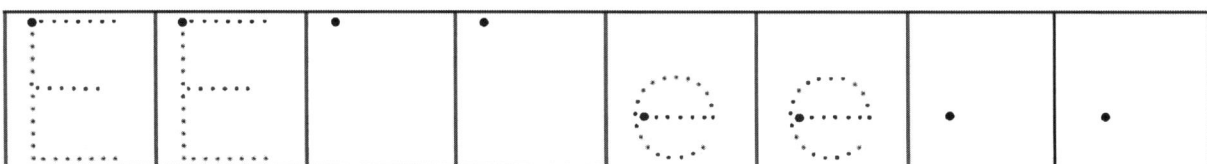

4) Copy this sentence on the line and read it out loud:

E is for exit.

My name is _____ .

Favorite Book

Directions: Draw pictures and label by ear spelling in the boxes below.

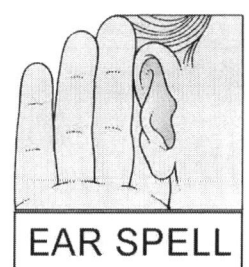
EAR SPELL

This is the cover of my favorite book:

(Title of the book)

Continue on next page.

7.4 - Letter Ee

_____

_____ is my favorite book because:

Name _____.

Following Directions: Short e

1) Find and color the egg blue.
2) Find and color the web blue.
3) Find and color the elf blue.
4) Find and color the jet blue.
5) Find and color the bed blue.

My name is _____.

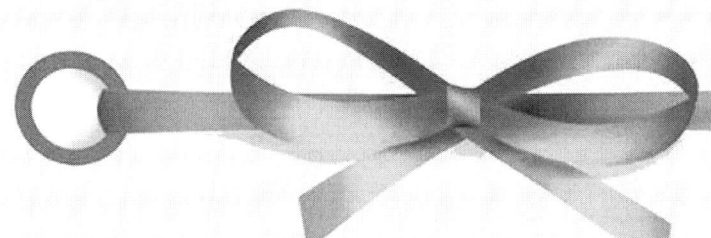

Wrap it up!

1) Choose one plural word to complete the sentence.
2) Write the sentence on the lines below.
3) Draw a picture for your sentence in the box.

WORD BANK:
eggs
elephants
eggplants
engines
emeralds
envelopes

I can find the _____.

My name is _____ .

1) Follow the model and finger trace **F** and **f**, then read the sentence aloud.

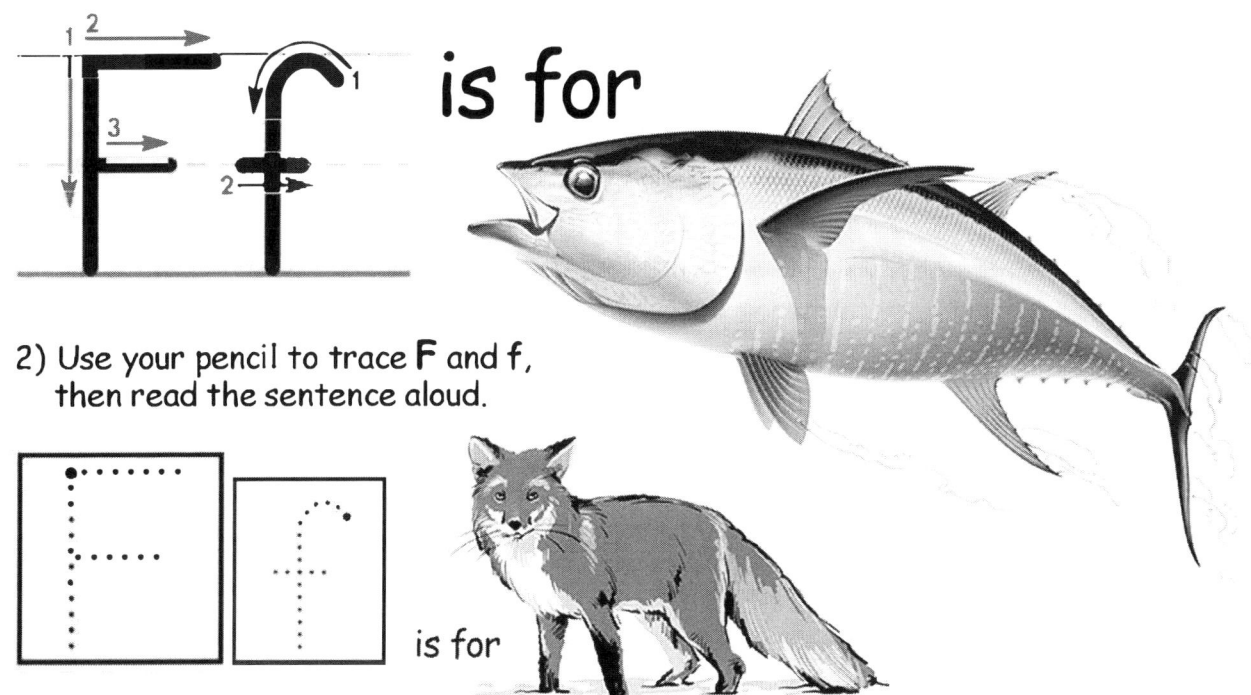

is for

2) Use your pencil to trace **F** and **f**, then read the sentence aloud.

is for

3) Use your pencil to trace the letters in the boxes then start at the dots and write your own.

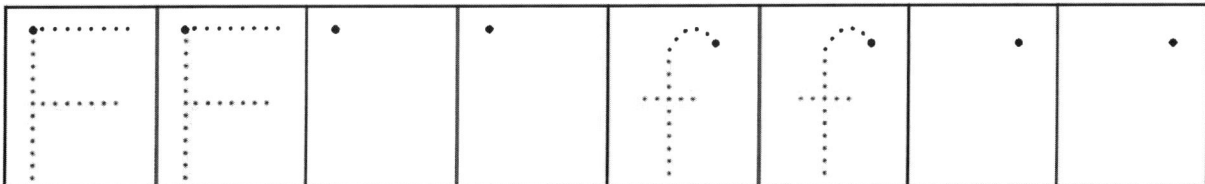

4) Copy this sentence on the line and read it out loud:

F is for five.

8.1 - Letter Ff

Complete Sentences Worksheet

Example:

	describing word (adjective)	who or what (noun)	did what (verb)	where? or when?
The	happy	dog	jumps	at the park

The happy dog jumps at the park.

Go to next page.

	describing word (adjective)	who or what (noun)	did what (verb)	where? or when?
The				

8.5 - Letter Ff

My name is _____.

Choose a word that starts with **F** to complete the sentence below. Then write in on the lines and draw a picture in the box.

WORD BANK:

fish   **frog**   **ferret**
fox   **flamimgo**   **fly**

Wrap it up!

Look at the little _____ jump up.

My name is _____.

1) Follow the model and finger trace **D** and **d**, then read the sentence aloud.

is for

2) Use your pencil to trace **D** and **d**, then read the sentence aloud.

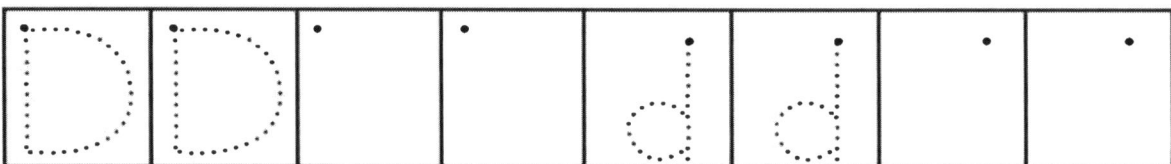

is for

3) Use your pencil to trace the letters in the boxes then start at the dots and write your own.

4) Copy this sentence on the line and read it out loud:

D is for dime.

Name _____.

Read the sentences and circle 👍 if it is a **complete sentence** and circle 👎 if it is not.

Find the Sentences!

 Come and.

 I see a big, blue dog.

 The can.

 I can jump up!

9.4 - Letter Dd

Name _____

What balloon animal do you want the clown to make for you?

Write your own complete sentence by **ear spelling** and draw a picture of your balloon animal in the box.

My name is _____.

Wrap it up!

1) Choose a word from the word bank to complete the sentence.
2) Write the sentence on the lines below.
3) Draw a picture for your sentence in the box.
4) Underline your sight words.

WORD BANK:
dog   donkey
dinosaur   duck
deer   dingo
dolphin

Can you make the _____ go away from me?

9.5 - Letter Dd

44

My name is _____ .

1) Follow the model and finger trace **G** and **g**, then read the sentence aloud.

Gg is for

2) Use your pencil to trace **G** and **g**, then read the sentence aloud.

Gg is for

3) Use your pencil to trace the letters in the boxes then start at the dots and write your own.

4) Copy this sentence on the line and read it out loud:

G is for girl and goat.

Write a Sentence!

Example:

	describing word (adjective)	who or what (noun)	did what (verb)	where? or when?
The	happy	gerbil	flies	up.

The happy gerbil flies up.

Name _____

	describing word (adjective)	who or what (noun)	did what (verb)	where? or when?
The				

10.4 - Letter Gg

My name is _____.

MAKING CONNECTIONS

When I read this in the story,

and shape art in Word

It reminds me of ...

Text

to

Self

47   10.5 - Letter Gg

My name is _____.

1) Fill in the blank with a word that starts with a letter from the bank. Write the sentence on the lines.
2) Draw a picture for your sentence in the box.
3) Underline your sight words with a yellow line.

Wrap it up!

Word Bank:
goat
gerbil
gorilla
goose
gopher
guinea pig
giraffe

I do not see one _____ in my garden.

10.5 - Letter Gg

My name is _____ .

1) Follow the model and finger trace **I** and **i**, then read the sentence aloud.

I is for insect

2) Use your pencil to trace **I** and **i**, then read the sentence aloud.

i is for iguana

3) Use your pencil to trace the letters in the boxes then start at the dots and write your own.

4) Copy this sentence on the line and read it out loud:

I is for igloo.

49   11.1 - Letter Ii

Name _____.

Expanding Sentences

Directions: Expand the sentences by filling in the blanks with words from the word bank.

Sentences	Word Bank
The frog jumps.	
The _____ frog jumps.	little
The _____ frog jumps _____ .	little up
The _____ frog jumps _____ and _____ .	little up down

Sentences	Word Bank
The cat comes.	
The _____ cat comes.	big
The _____ cat comes _____ _____ .	big and plays
The _____ cat comes _____ _____ _____ _____ .	big and plays with me

11.4 - Letter Ii   50

My name is _____.

Choose a word that starts with **i** to complete the sentence below. Then write in on the lines and draw a picture in the box.

Wrap it up!

WORD BANK:

iguana   **insect**   **impala**

You can play with the _____.

My name is _____ .

1) Follow the model and finger trace **L** and **l**, then read the sentence aloud.

is for

2) Use your pencil to trace **L** and **l**, then read the sentence aloud.

is for

3) Use your pencil to trace the letters in the boxes then start at the dots and write your own.

4) Copy this sentence on the line and read it out loud:

L is for lab.

12.1 - Letter Ll

Name _____.

Act it out!

Act out each **verb**. Each number has similar words with different meanings.

1. Ways to move: walk, march, strut, prance

2. Ways to say things: talk, babble, whisper, yell

3. Ways to eat: lick, chew swallow, chomp, nibble

4. Ways to dance: leap, twirl, glide, twist, shake

My name is _____.

Sight Word Practice

Write all of these sentences on the lines below.
Then read them out loud.

Jump in and play with me!

I can find a little one with you.

Do not look away.

I can make my lunch.

Popcorn Sight Words Game

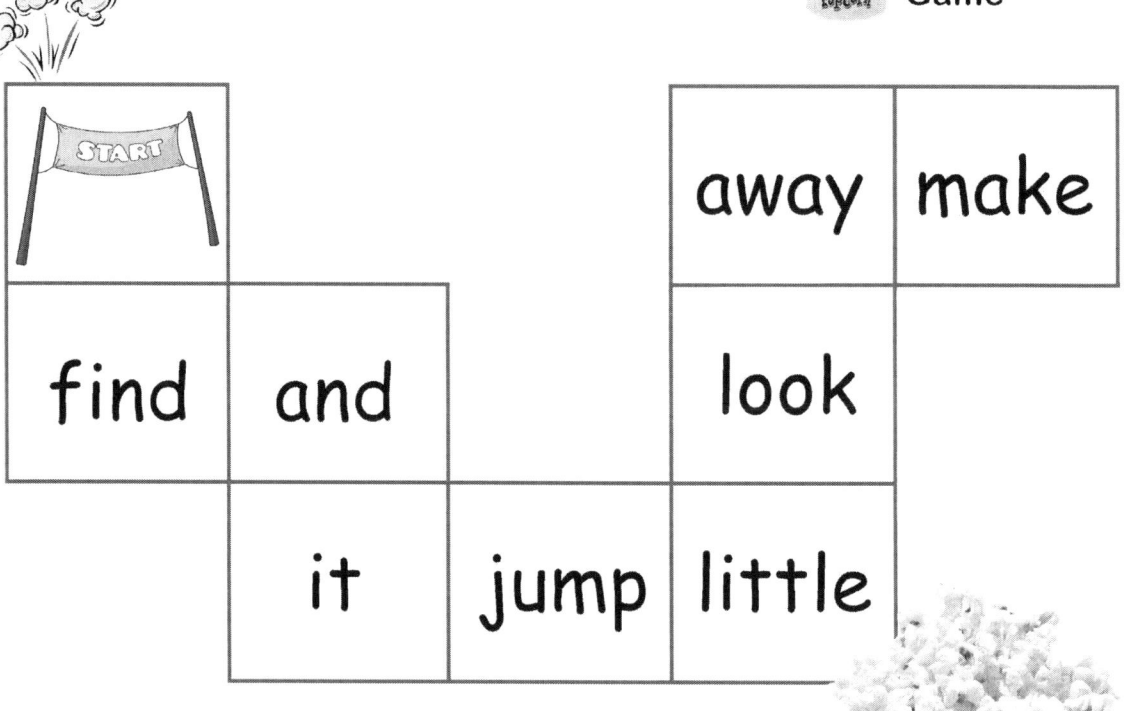

Popcorn Sight Words Game

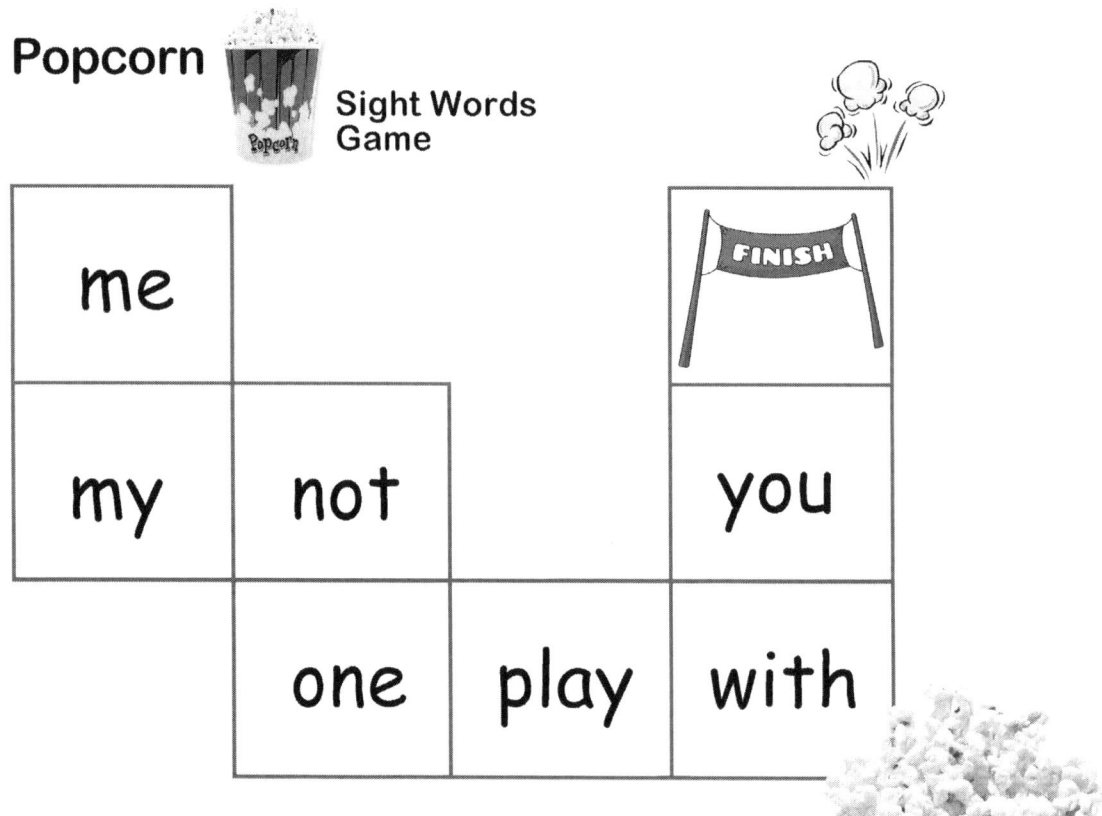

55   12.3 - Letter Ll

Name _____ .

L Sight Words

Make Sentences

Make your own sentence on the lines below using your **L** sight words. Don't forget the punctuation mark at the end.

Copy your sentence on the lines and start the first word with a capital letter.

Your **L** sight words are on the following pages.

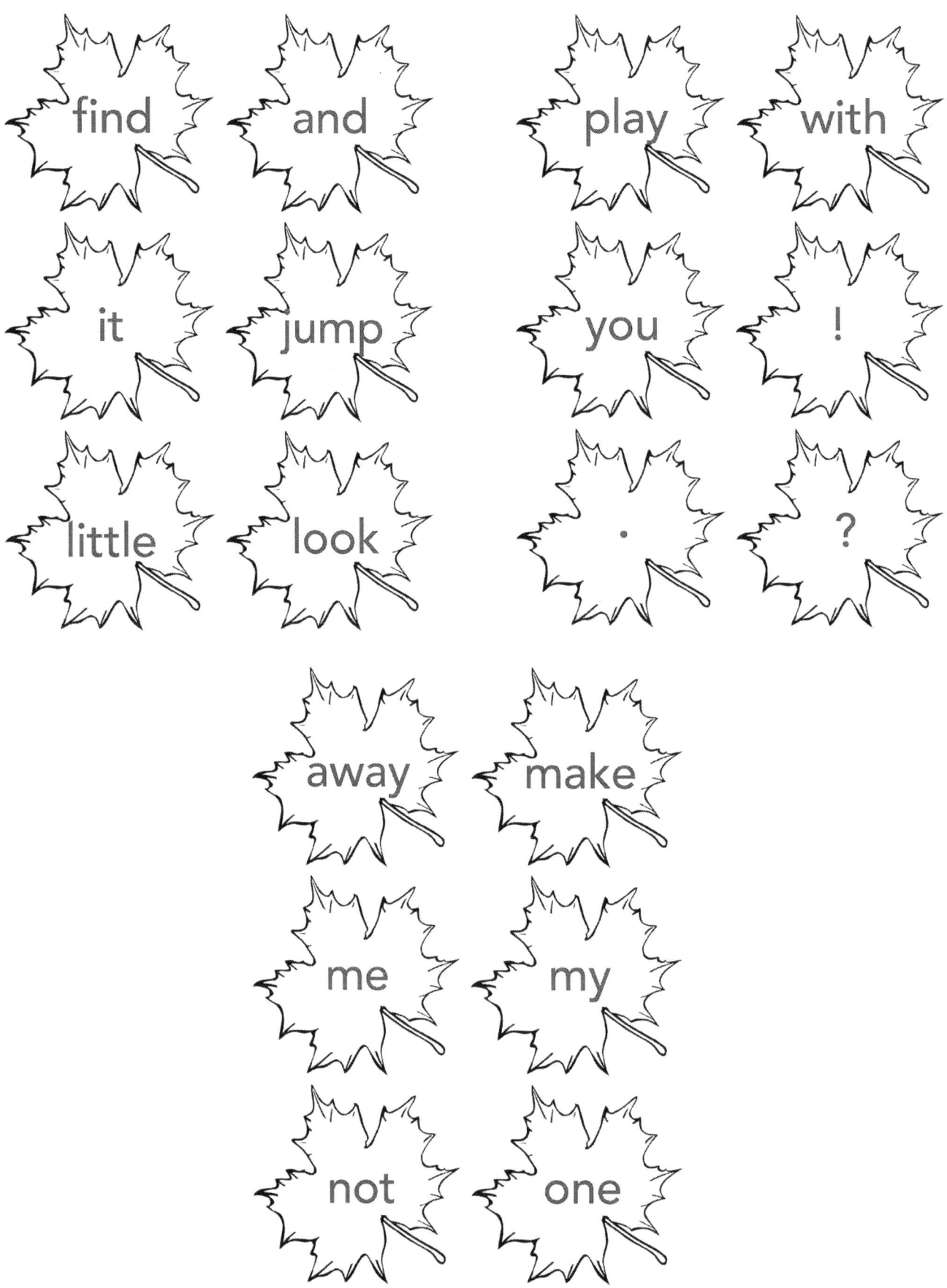

My name is _____.

MAKING CONNECTIONS

In the empty storybook page, draw a picture about a part of the Module story you can relate to (favorite part of the story). Then in the thought bubble, draw another picture of another story you have read in your daily life that you can make a connection with.

Text to Text

it reminded me of this story.

12.5 - Letter Ll

My name is _____.

Missing Letters

Trace the missing letters:

It is a party!

I see a gift, a little girl with an envelope, and a giraffe with dots.

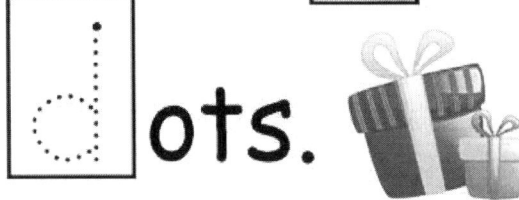

My name is _____ .

1) Follow the model and finger trace **C** and **c**, then read the sentence aloud.

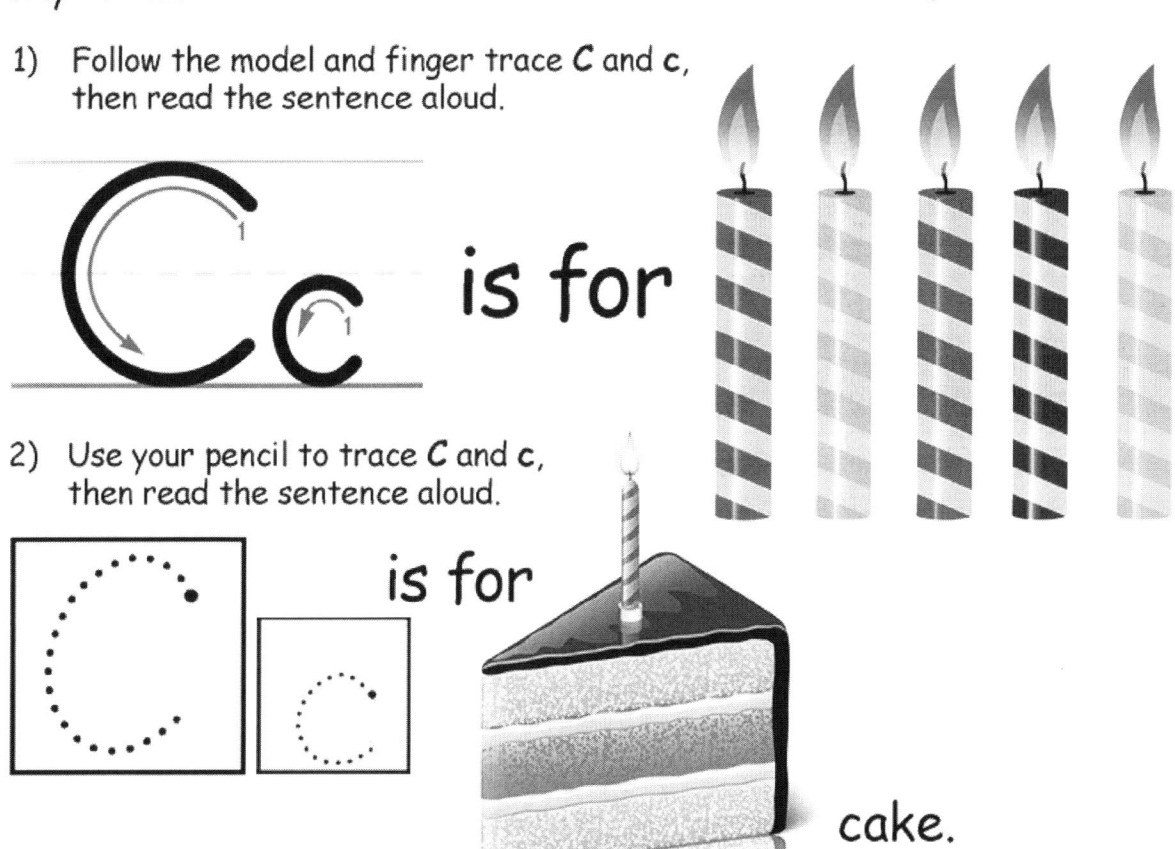

Cc is for cake.

2) Use your pencil to trace **C** and **c**, then read the sentence aloud.

3) Use your pencil to trace the letters in the boxes then start at the dots and write your own.

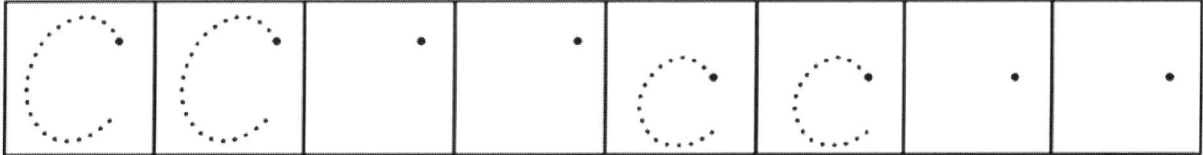

4) Copy this sentence on the line below:

C is for cat.

13.1 - Letter Cc

My name is _____.

Words in My World

Directions:
Look at the question and draw a picture for your answer. Label it by ear spelling.

 Who do you know that is funny?

 What do you think is scary?

 What makes you happy?

 What is your dream?

My Favorite Part
Independent Reading Book

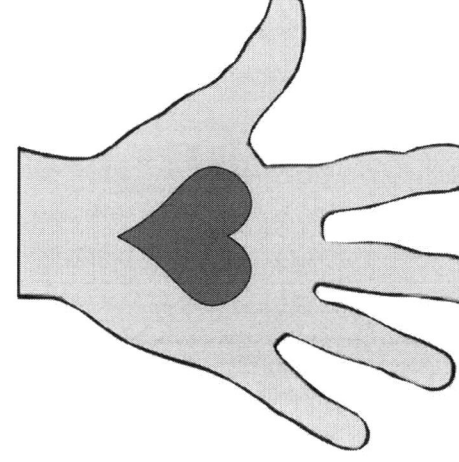

Select one of the following activities for this assignment.

1. Complete the following page, drawing a picture of your favorite part of the story you read.

2. Build your favorite part of the story with blocks, Legos, or other building materials. Take a photo to turn into your teacher.

3. Act out your favorite part of the story while a parent records you on a device (phone, tablet, computer web camera, etc.). Turn your video clip into your teacher.

Continue on the next page.

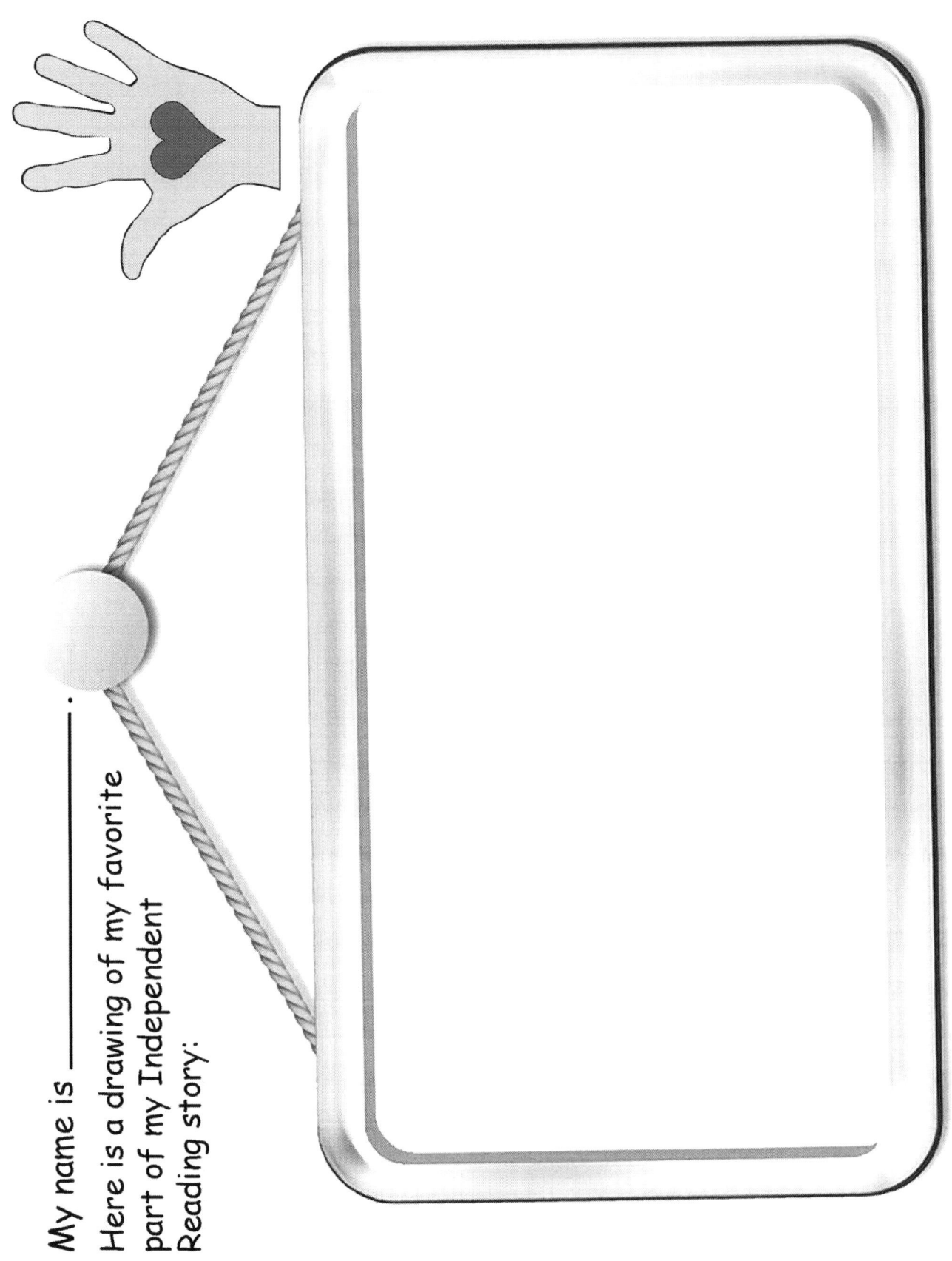

My name is _____.

Here is a drawing of my favorite part of my Independent Reading story:

My name is _____.

Wrap it up!

1) Draw a picture for each sight word and write the word under the picture.
2) Choose a word that starts with **c** in the last box and draw its picture.
3) Write the **c** word that you drew under the picture.

| up | three | to | c word |

13.5 - Letter Cc

My name is _____.

1) Follow the model and finger trace P and p, then read the sentence aloud.

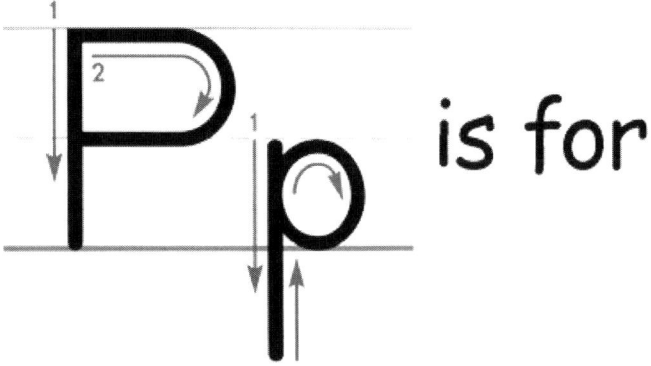 is for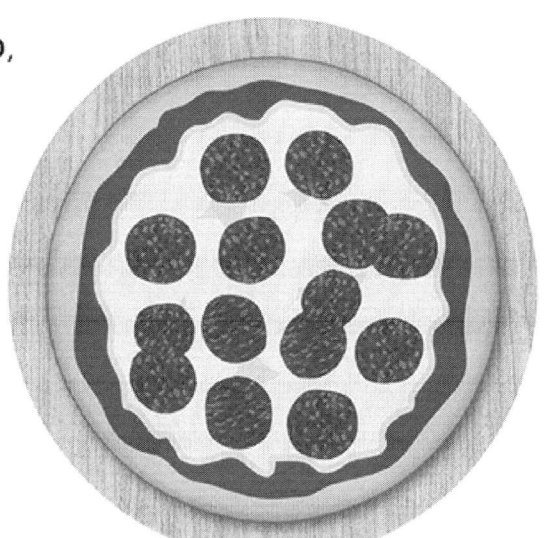

2) Use your pencil to trace P and p, then read the sentence aloud.

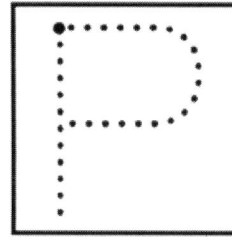 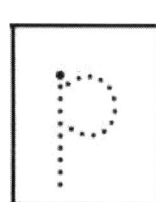 is for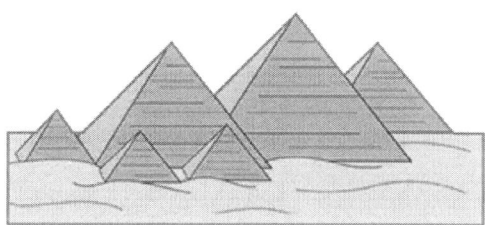

3) Use your pencil to trace the letters in the boxes then start at the dots and write your own.

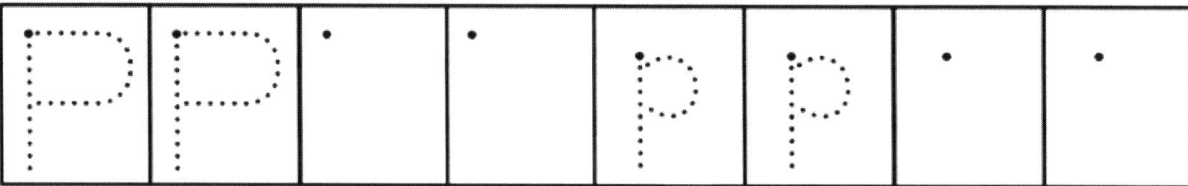

4) Copy this sentence on the line below:

P is for penny.

Writing Web: Characters

Choose a character from a favorite book, an Independent Reading story, or a weekly story. Then select one of the following activities for this assignment.

1. Complete the following page to creating a Character Web.

2. Create a puppet (paper bag or stick) of the character. Take a photo to turn into your teacher.

3. Dress up as the character and tell 1-2 facts about yourself as the character while a parent records you on a device (phone, tablet, computer web camera, etc.). Turn your video clip into your teacher.

Example:

Here is an example of a Web with **Little Red Riding Hood**. Your assignment is on the next page.

Continue on the next page.

14.5 - Letter Pp

My name is _____.

1. Choose any character as the topic for your writing web. You could choose a character from a favorite book, an Independent Reading story, or a weekly story.

2. Draw a picture of the character in the middle circle and label it by ear spelling.

3. Think of four details to describe the character. Draw a picture in each circle and label your pictures with ear spelling.

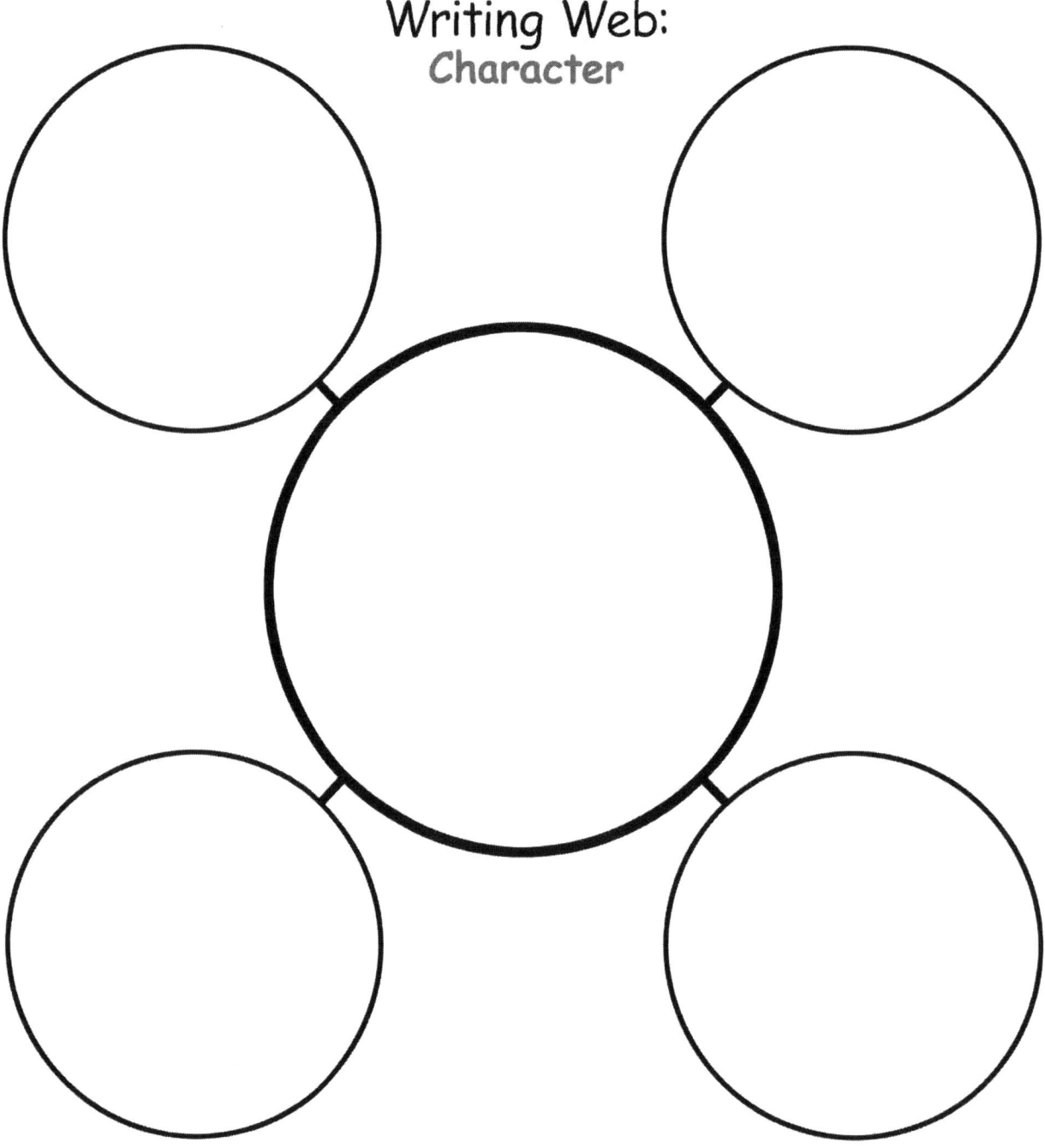

Writing Web: Character

My name is _____.

Wrap it up!

1) Draw a picture for each sight word and write the word under the picture.
2) Choose a word that starts with **p** in the last box and draw its picture.
3) Ear spell the **p** word under the picture you drew.

two	where	we	p words

14.5 - Letter Pp

My name is _____ .

1) Follow the model and finger trace **R** and **r**, then read the sentence aloud.

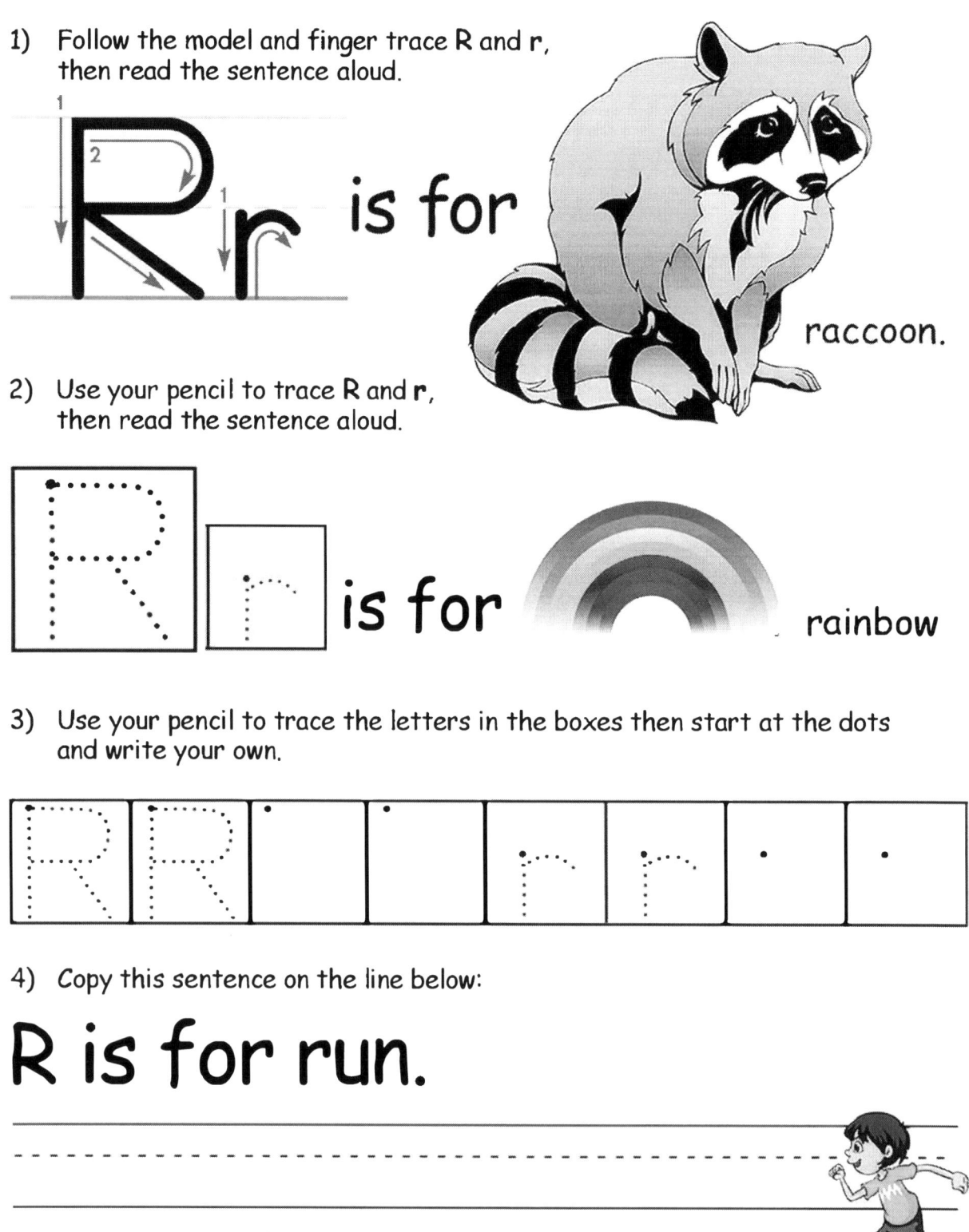

Rr is for raccoon.

2) Use your pencil to trace **R** and **r**, then read the sentence aloud.

Rr is for rainbow

3) Use your pencil to trace the letters in the boxes then start at the dots and write your own.

4) Copy this sentence on the line below:

R is for run.

My name is _____.

Setting Match

Draw a line from the picture to the setting where it can be found.

rose

raft

raccoon

rainbow

river

sky

garden

forest

15.4 - Letter Rr

Setting

Choose a favorite book, an Independent Reading story, or a weekly story. Then select **one** of the following activities for this assignment about setting.

1. Complete the following page by drawing and labeling the setting.

2. Create the setting with items from your home or your yard. Take a photo to turn into your teacher.

3. Find a picture on the computer or in a magazine of the setting. Describe and tell about the setting while a parent records you on a device (phone, tablet, computer web camera, etc.). Turn the video clip into your teacher.

Continue on the next page.

My name is _____.

Wrap it up!

1) Draw a picture for each sight word and write the word under the picture.
2) Choose a word that starts with **r** in the last box and draw its picture.
3) Ear spell the **r** word under the picture you drew.

am	red	yellow	r words

15.5 - Letter Rr

My name is _____.

1) Follow the model and finger trace O and o, then read the sentence aloud.

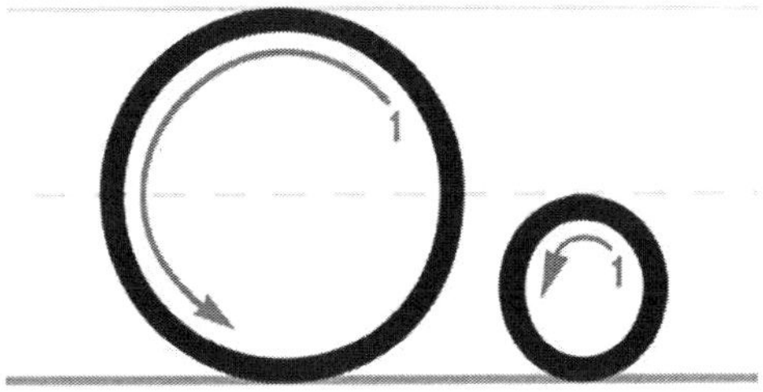

is for

2) Use your pencil to trace O and o, then read the sentence aloud.

is for

oranges.

3) Use your pencil to trace the letters in the boxes then start at the dots and write your own.

4) Copy this sentence on the line below:

O is for on and off.

16.1 - Letter Oo

Parts of a Book

My name is _____.

1. Circle the title (name of the book) with a blue crayon.
2. Underline the author's name in a red crayon.
3. Underline the illustrator's name in a yellow crayon.
4. Draw a smiley face on the back cover.

Title Page

When you open a book, the first page is called the title page. It tells you the information from the front cover and also the publisher's name and date when the book was first printed. Locate the publisher's name and date and circle it with a red crayon.

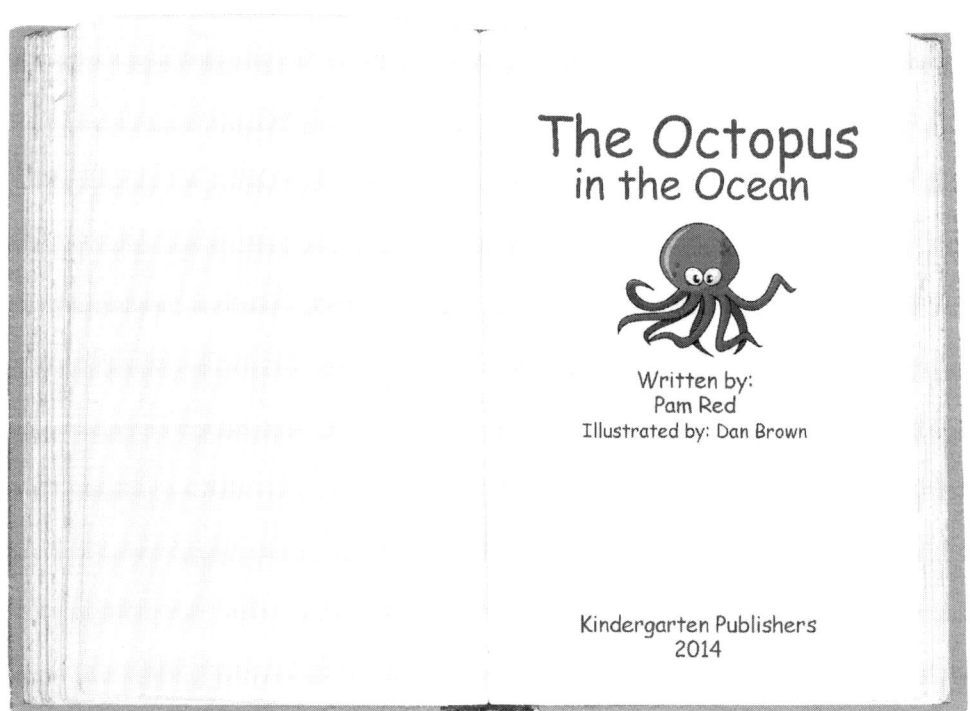

Make Your Own Book Cover

1. Write a title (name for your book) on the front cover.
2. Write your name as the author.
3. Write your name as the illustrator.
4. Draw a picture of what the book is about.

Written by:

Illustrated by:

16.2 - Letter Oo

 My name is _____.

Labeling Events

SPELL

Directions:
Label the events of the story, "**Where Are the Oranges?**" by ear spelling.

1) Look at the picture of the word you are to label.

2) Say the word out loud and listen to the sounds.

3) Ear spell the word by writing any letters you know for the sounds of the word on the line.

Beginning:

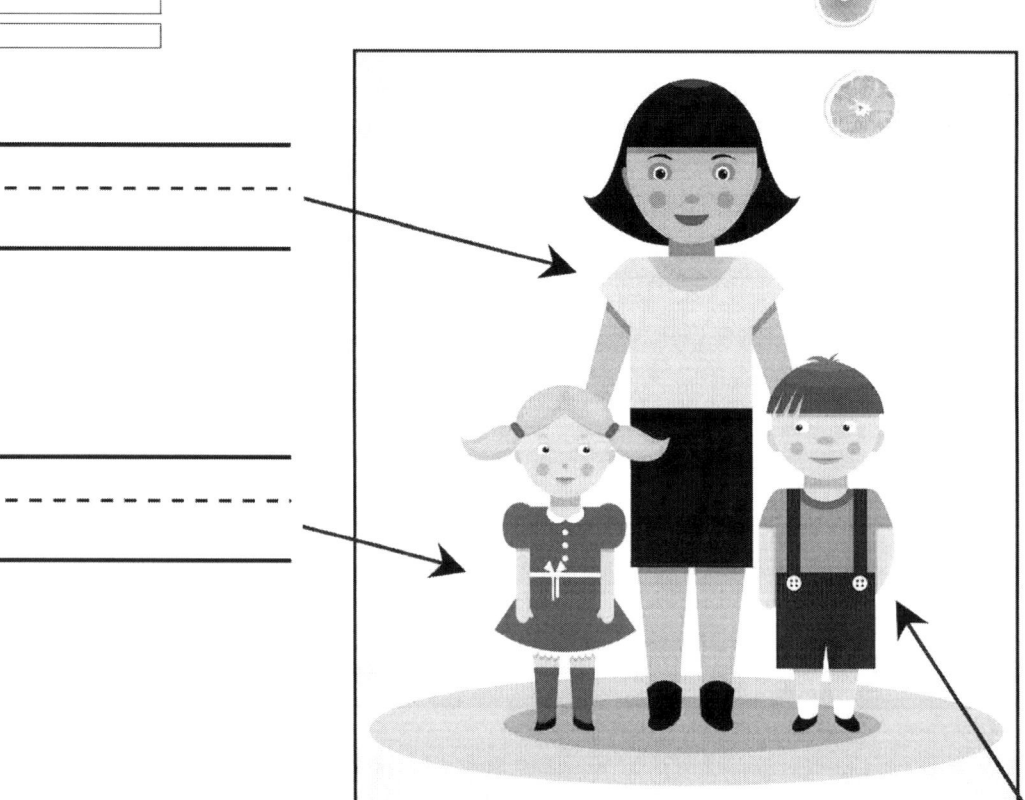

Continue on the next page.

77   16.4 - Letter Oo

Middle:

End:

16.4 - Letter Oo

Story Events

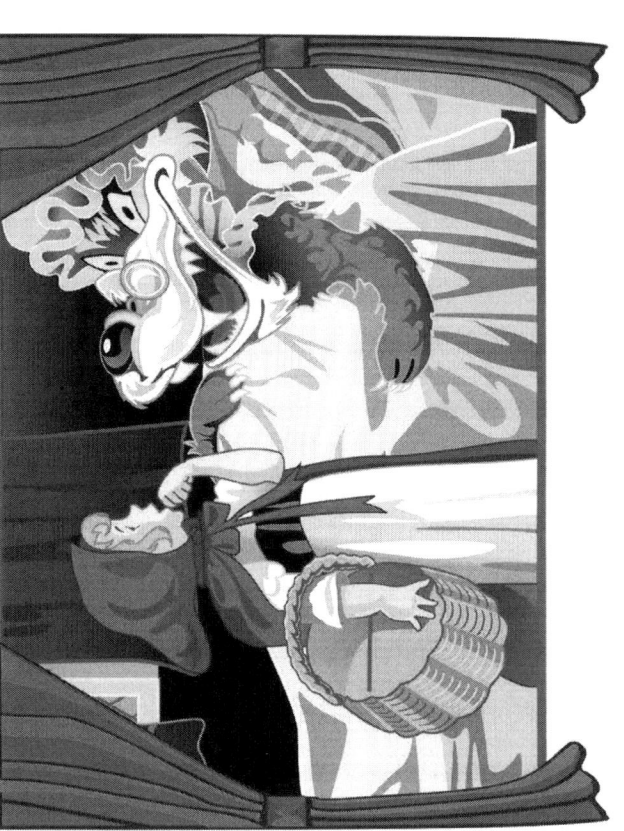

Choose a favorite book, an Independent Reading story, or a weekly story. Then select **one** of the following activities for this assignment about story events.

1. Complete the following page by drawing and labeling what happened in the beginning, middle and end.

2. Create the beginning, middle, and ending events with Legos, dolls, stuffed animals, etc. Take one photo of each (3 total) to turn into your teacher.

3. Act out the beginning, middle, and ending events while an adult records you on a device (phone, tablet, computer web camera, etc.). Turn the video clip into your teacher.

Continue on the next page.

My name is _____.

Story Events

1. Draw a picture of what happened in the beginning of the story. Ear spell one word from your picture and write it on the line.
2. Draw a picture of what happened in the middle of the story. Ear spell one word from your picture and write it on the line.
3. Draw a picture of what happened at the end of the story. Ear spell one word from your picture and write it on the line.

Beginning	Middle	End

My name is _____.

Wrap it up!
1) Draw a picture for each sight word and write the word under the picture.
2) Choose a word that starts with **o** in the last box and draw its picture.
3) Ear spell the **o** word under the picture you drew.

eat	ate	did	**o** words

My name is _____ .

1) Follow the model and finger trace H and h, then read the sentence aloud.

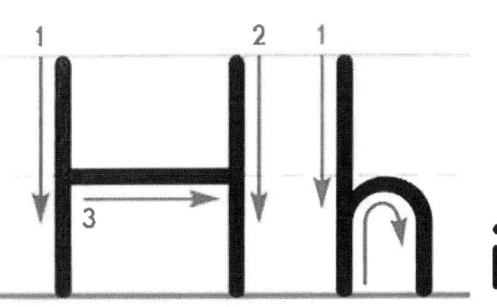 is for

2) Use your pencil to trace H and h, then read the sentence aloud.

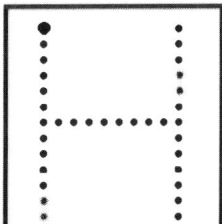 is for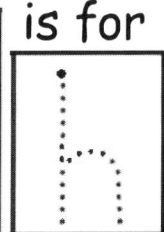

3) Use your pencil to trace the letters in the boxes then start at the dots and write your own.

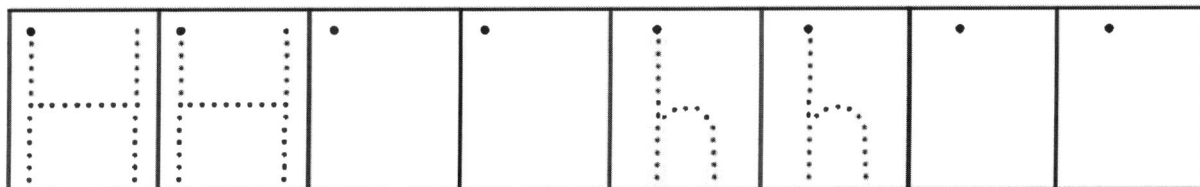

4) Copy this sentence on the line below:

H is for hug.

_____

_____

My name is _____.

It's Matching Time!

Draw a line from the problem on the left to its solution on the right.

 Problem:	Solution: 

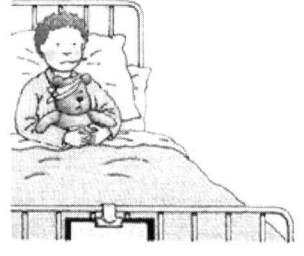

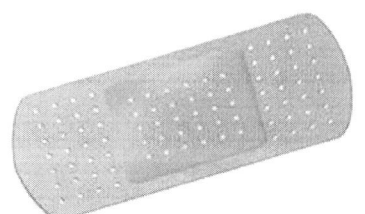

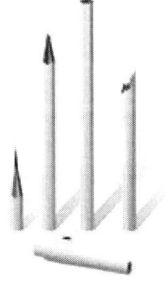

17.4 - Letter Hh

My name is _____.

Problem and Solution Activity

| Problem:  | Solution:  |

Select **one** of the following activities for this assignment about the problem from, "**Help Me Find My Horse**" and its solution.

1. Complete the following page by drawing and labeling the problem and solution.

2. Create a puppet of the brown horse with black hair, the boy, and the girl. Take photos and email them to your teacher.

3. Act out the problem and solution while an adult records you on a device (phone, tablet, computer web camera, etc.). Turn the video clip into your teacher.

Continue on the next page.

My name is _____.

1. Draw a picture of the problem from, "**Help Me Find My Horse**." Ear spell one word from your picture and write it on the line.

2. Draw a picture of the solution from, "**Help Me Find My Horse**." Ear spell one word from your picture and write it on the line.

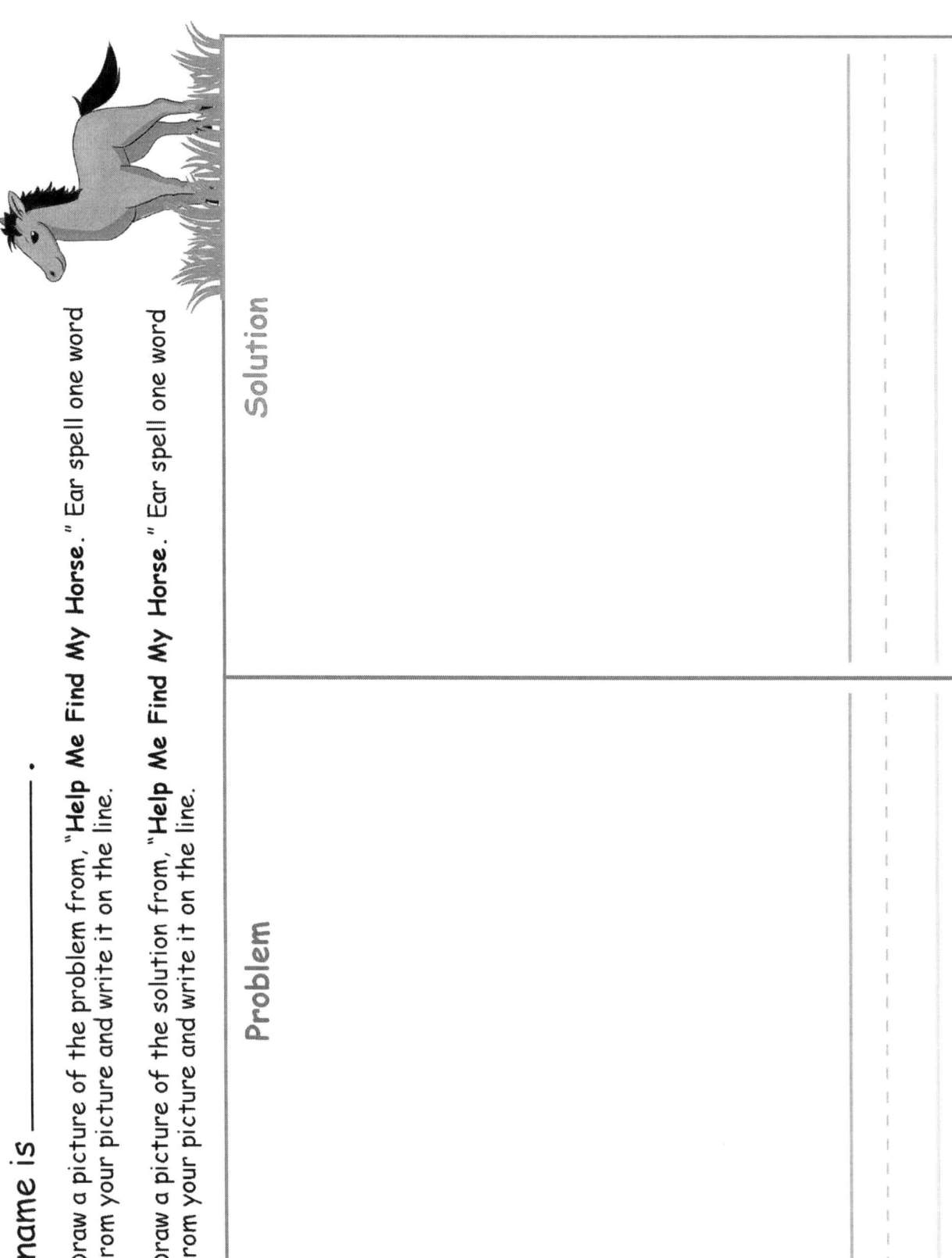

Problem

Solution

My name is _____.

Wrap it up!

1) Draw a picture for each sight word and write the word under the picture.
2) Choose a word that starts with **h** and draw its picture.
3) Ear spell the **h** word under the picture you drew.

brown	black	help	h word

17.5 - Letter Hh

My name is _____.

1) Follow the model and finger trace **V** and **v**, then read the sentence aloud.

Vv is for

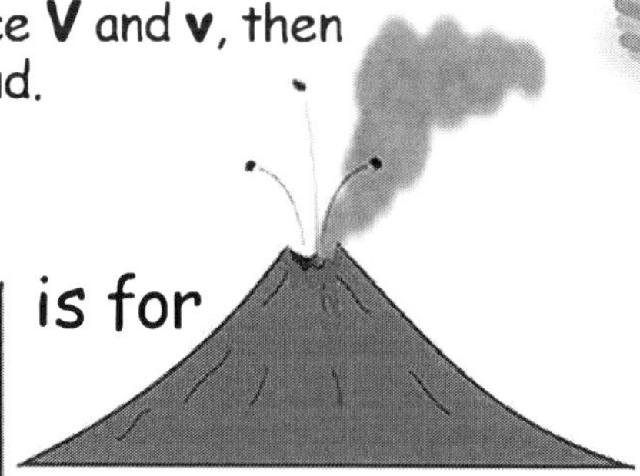

2) Use your pencil to trace **V** and **v**, then read the sentence aloud.

is for

3) Use your pencil to trace the letters in the boxes then start at the dots and write your own.

4) Copy this sentence on the line below:

V is for vet.

My name is _____.

Drawing Descriptions

Draw a picture in each box to represent the description.

The van is blue with yellow tires.

Continue on the next page.

18.2 - Letter Vv

The volcano is big and the lava is red.

I see a happy vet with a pet.

Continue on the next page.

I see a tall boy playing the violin.

My name is _____.

Sight Word Practice

Write all of these sentences on the lines below. Then read them out loud.

I am two.

I can go up to three.

I am yellow, black and brown.

Continue on the following page.

Where can I eat?

Did you help?

We ate red bell peppers.

Popcorn Sight Words Game

yellow	am
where	
we	two
to	up
three	

START

Popcorn
Sight Words Game

red	did
	eat	ate

	eat	ate	help	black
FINISH	brown			

18.3 - Letter Vv

Main Idea

Choose a favorite book, an Independent Reading story, or a weekly story. Then select **one** of the following activities for this assignment about story events.

1. Complete the following page by drawing and writing a sentence about the main idea.

2. Create the main idea with Legos, dolls, stuffed animals, etc. Then write the main idea in a sentence on a paper and put it in front. Take a photo and turn it into your teacher.

3. Act out the main idea while an adult records you on a device (phone, tablet, computer web camera, etc.). Turn the video clip into your teacher.

Continue on the next page.

My name is _____.

The title of the book I read or listened to is:

Book Title: _____

The main idea of the book is:

Main Idea

18.5 - Letter Vv

My name is _____ .

Pizza Party!
Trace the missing letters:

The b[o]y and gi[r]l

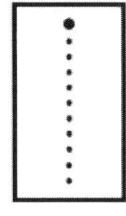
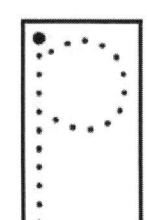

[l]ike to eat [p]izza and

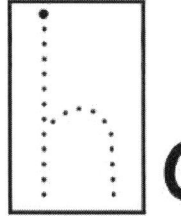

drink [h]ot [c]ocoa.

Cutout Worksheets

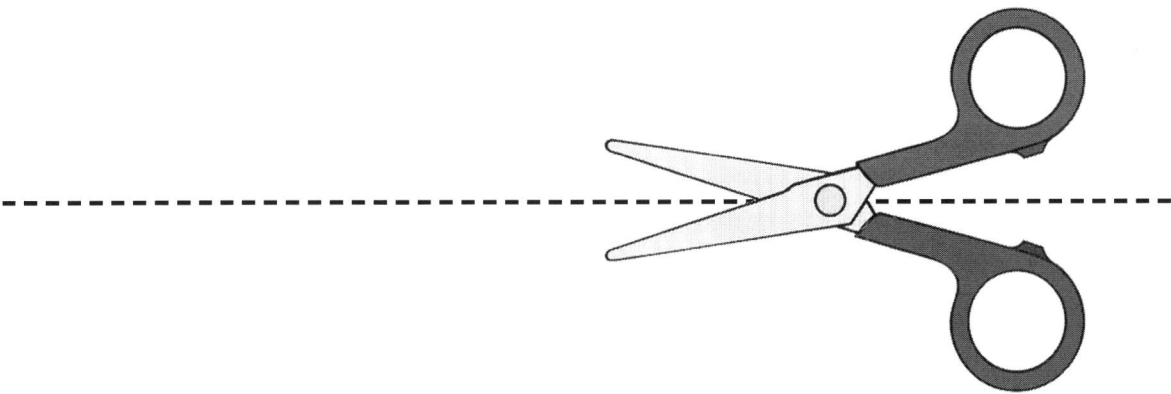

My name is _____.

Trace:

I see big

Color:

see big I

Write this sentence below: I see a big ant.

Cut out the letters below.
Glue them in these boxes to make your sight words.

☐   ☐☐☐   ☐☐☐

Cut Here

e s I i b g e

1.3 - Letter Aa

My name is _____.

Trace:

blue   a   can

Color:

a   blue   can

Write this sentence below: I see a blue can.

Cut out the letters below. Glue them in these boxes to make your sight words.

Cut Here

a a e u c n l b

2.3 - Letter Bb

My name is _____.

Trace:

said   the   in

Color: in said the

Write this sentence below: The big tiger said, "Roar!"

Cut out the letters below. Glue them in these boxes to make your sight words.

☐☐   ☐☐☐☐   ☐☐☐

Cut Here

i i s n t d a h e

3.3 - Letter Tt

My name is _____.

Draw what you did yesterday in the morning, afternoon, evening and night.

Morning	
Afternoon	
Evening	
Night	

Continue on next page.

Cut out the pictures at the bottom and glue them in chronological order.

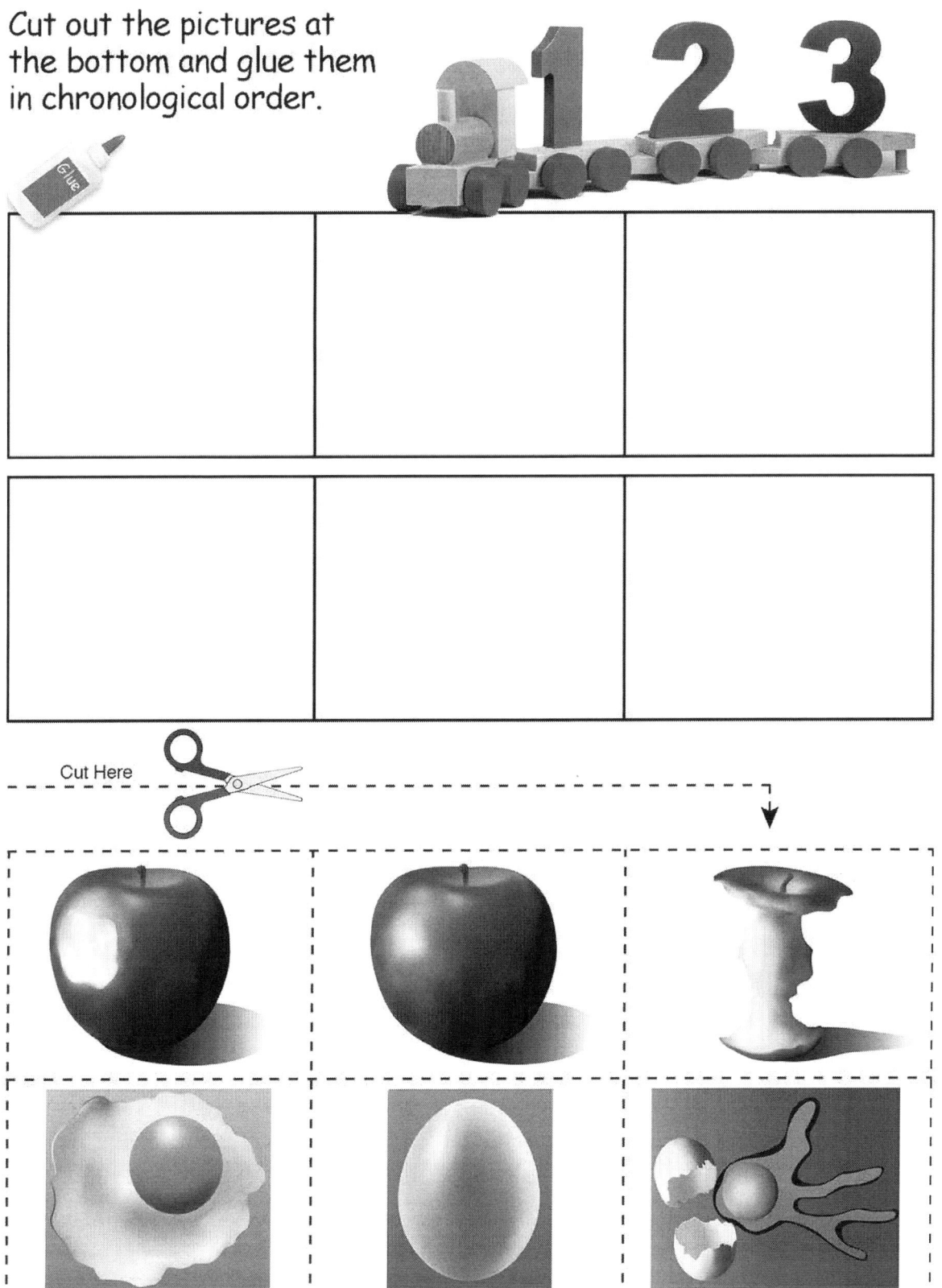

Cut Here

3.4 - Letter Tt

My name is _____.

Trace:

is   for   go

Color:

for   go   is

Write this sentence below: I can go for milk, it is good.

Cut out the letters below. Glue them in these boxes to make your sight words.

☐☐☐   ☐☐   ☐☐

Cut Here

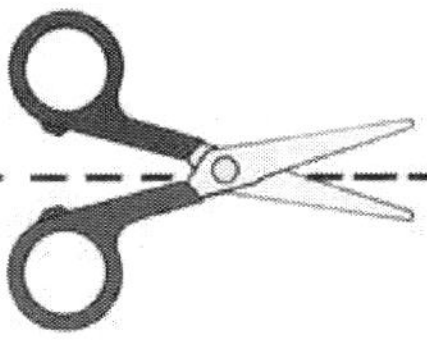

s r f o o g i

4.3 - Letter Mm

Cut out the events from the story, "Hungry Pets", and glue them on the second page in chronological order.

Continue on next page.

4.4 - Letter Mm

My name is _____.

Chronological Order

The Hungry Pets Glue the events of the story in chronological order into these numbered boxes.	1)
2)	3)
4)	5)
6)	7)
8)	9)

4.4 - Letter Mm

My name is _____.

??? Question Words ???
Who are you?

_____ are you?	_____ is soccer?
 I am the Teacher.	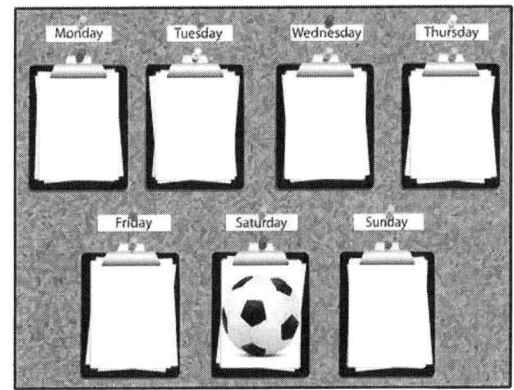 Soccer is Saturday.
_____ are you?	_____ is it?
 I am at the pet shop.	 It is a snake.

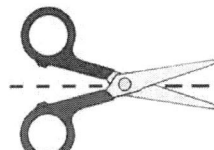 Cut out the words below and glue them into the correct sentences above.

| Who | What | When | Where |

Continue on next page.

_____ is swim class?	_____ are you eating?
Swim class is at 7:00.	I am hungry.
_____ are you?	_____ one is yours?
I am sad.	This doll is mine.

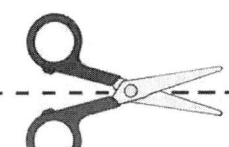

Cut out the words below and glue them into the correct sentences above.

| Why | How | Which | When |

5.2 - Letter Ss

 My name is _____ .

Trace:

come here down

Color:

come here down

Write this sentence below: Mom said, "Come down here."

Cut out the letters below. Glue them in these boxes to make your sight words.

Cut Here

r e e n c m e o o w h d

5.3 - Letter Ss

My name is ____________________.

Plurals - adding "s"

More Than One

Write the plural for each word by adding s. Then read each word out loud.

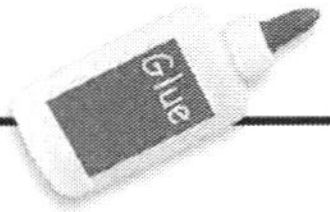

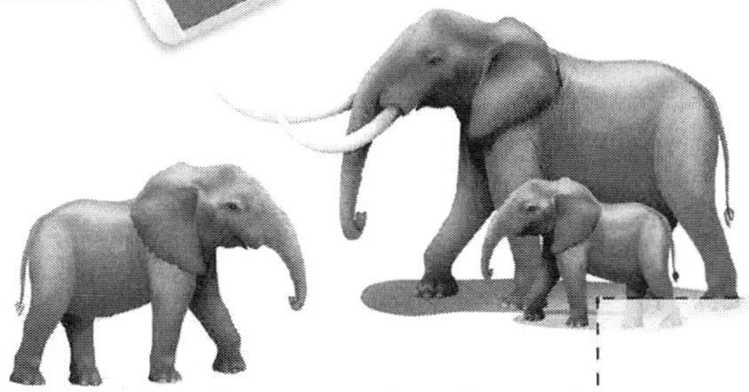

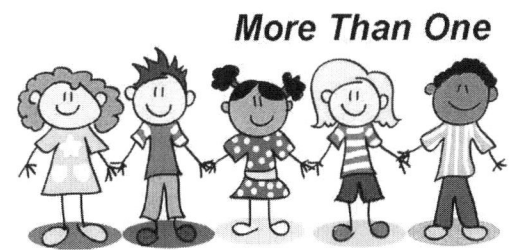

elephant elephant ☐

boy boy ☐

cat cat ☐

girl girl ☐

dog dog ☐

student student ☐

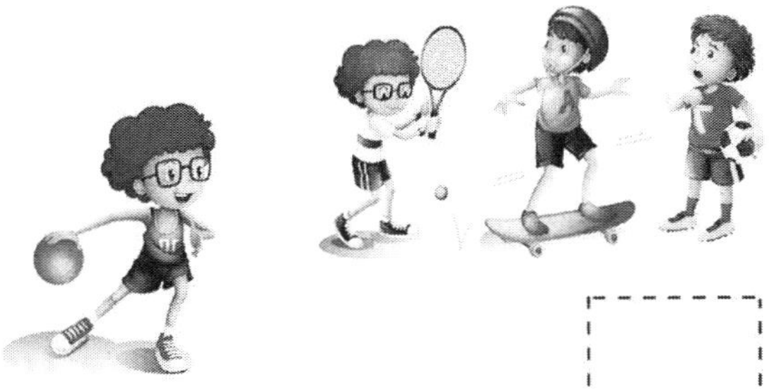

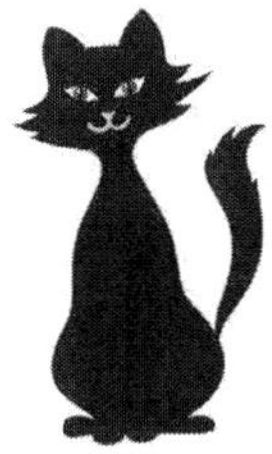

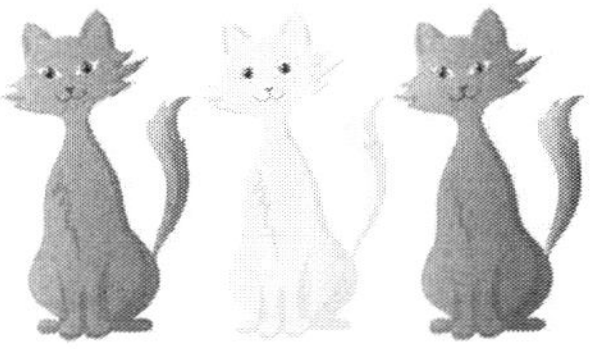

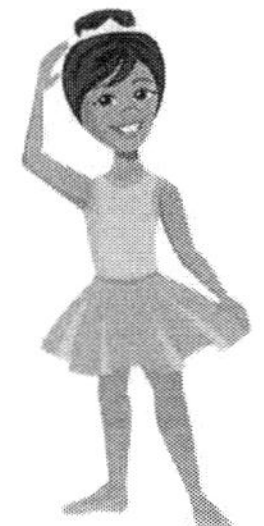

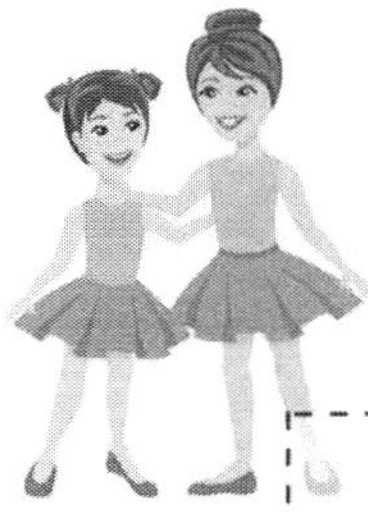

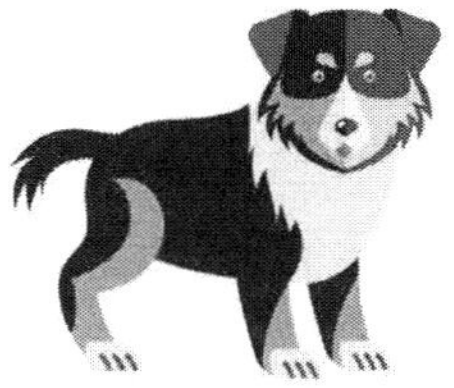

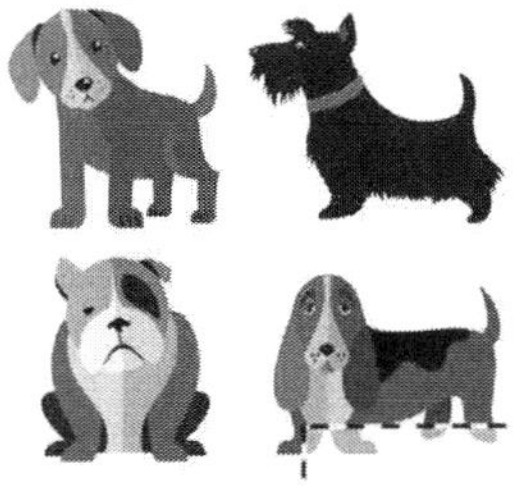

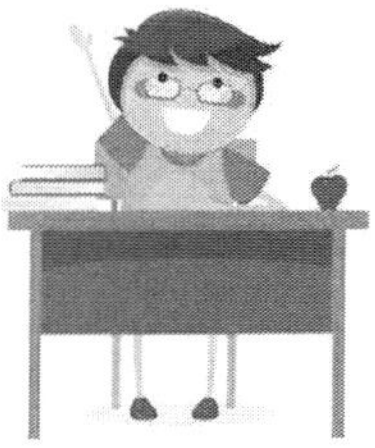

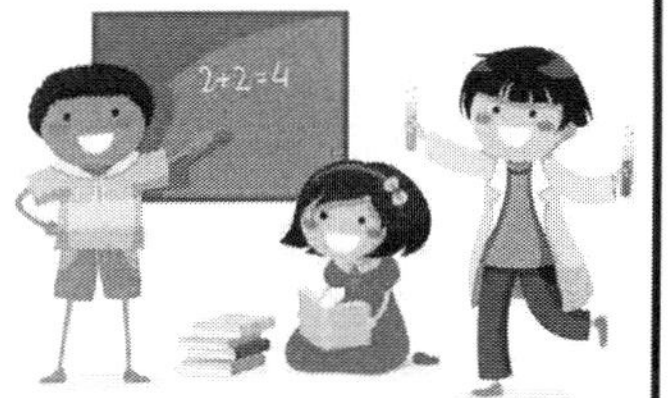

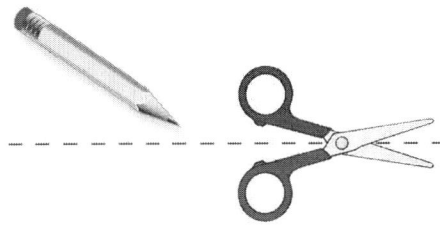

Trace each letter. Cut them out and glue them in the boxes above.

s s s s s s

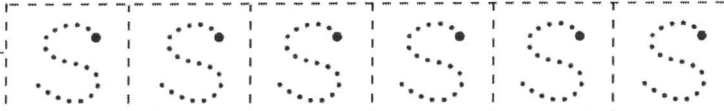

Continue on next page.

Plurals - adding "es"

Write the plural for each word by adding es. Then read each word out loud.

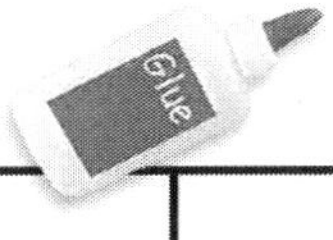

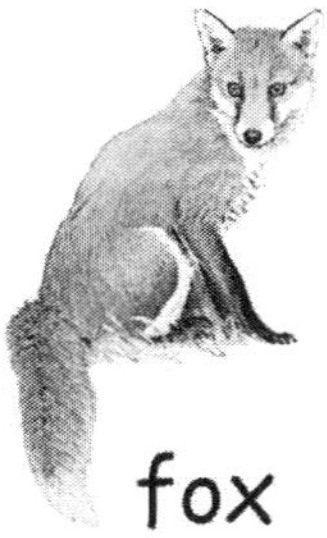

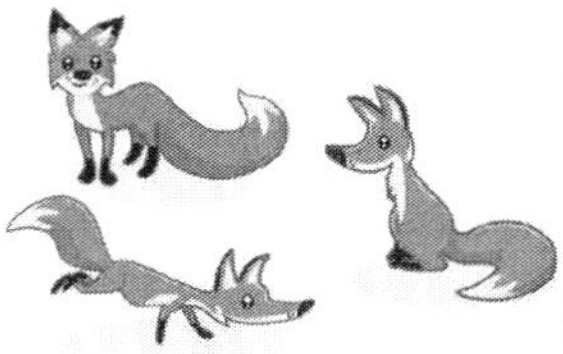

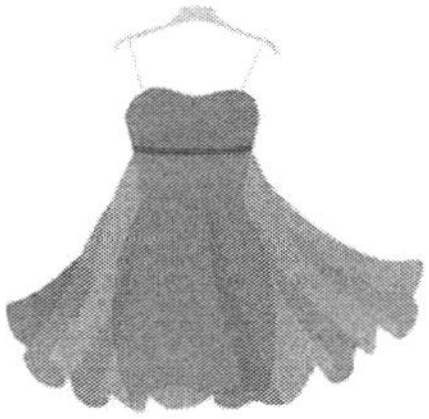

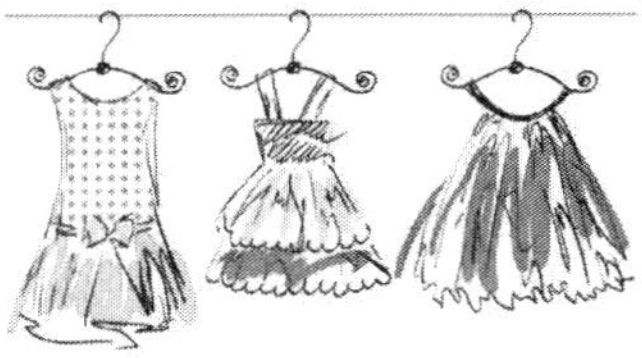

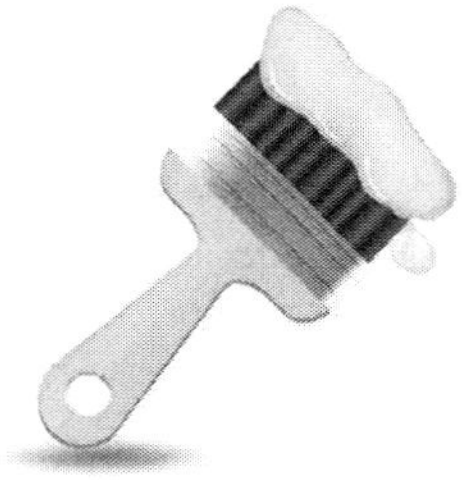

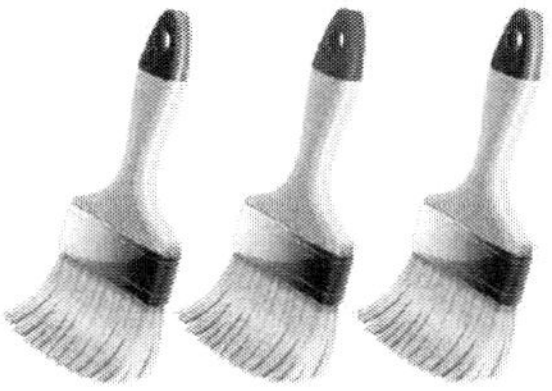

fox fox

dress dress

brush brush

watch watch

bus bus

box box

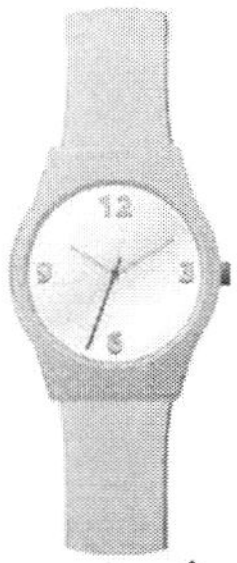

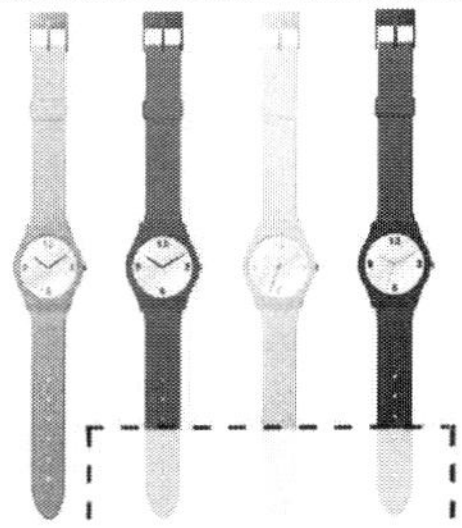

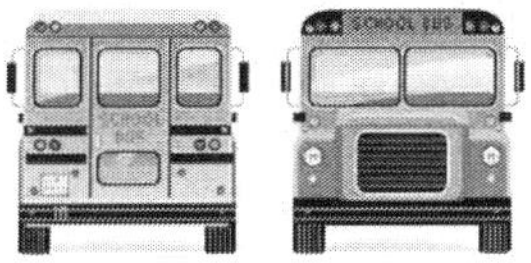

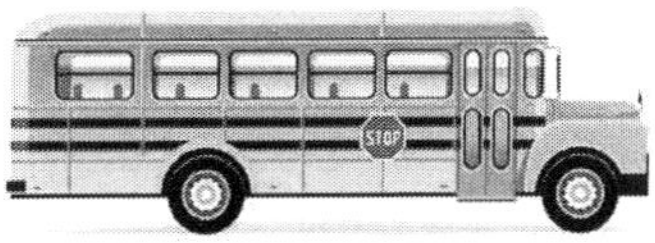

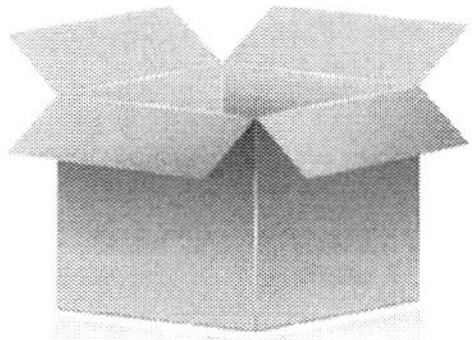

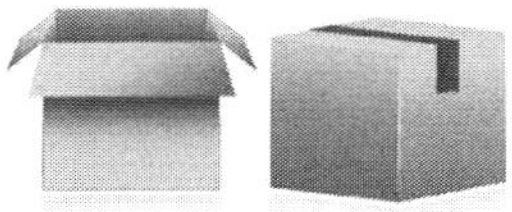

Trace each letter. Cut them out and glue them in the boxes above.

es es es es es es

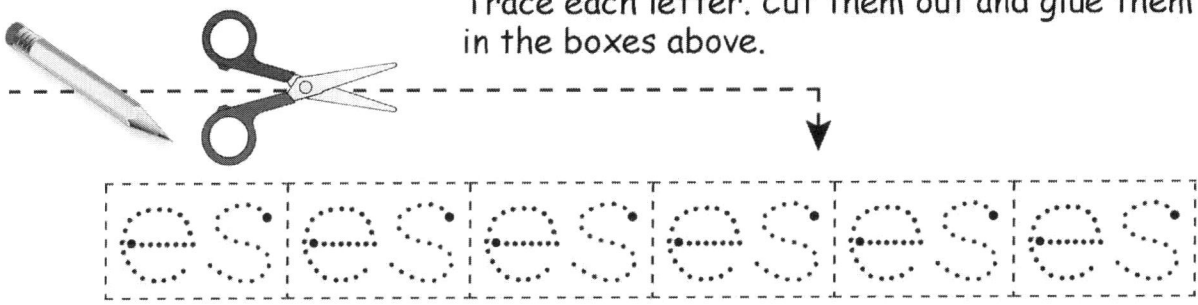

My name is _____.

Trace:

and it find

Color:

it find and

Write this sentence below: I see it and I can find it!

Cut out the letters below. Glue them in these boxes to make your sight words.

Cut Here

a d t i d n f n i

7.3 - Letter Ee

My name is _____.   # Punctuation

Read each sentence. Cut and glue the correct punctuation mark at the end.

A telling sentence ends with a **period**. [.]

A question sentence ends with a **question mark**. [?]

A sentence with emotion ends with an **exclamation point**. [!]

Is it blue [ ]

Hurry and jump in [ ]

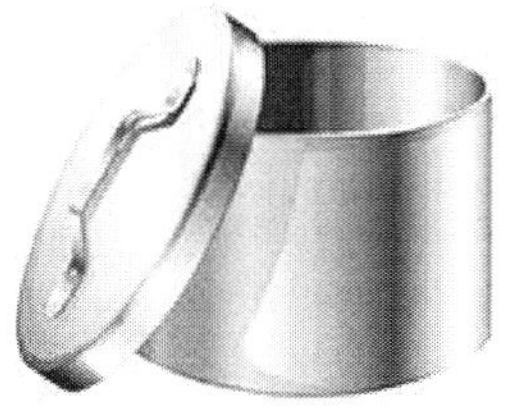

Is it in the can [ ]

I can see it [ ]

Come down here [ ]

Can it jump [ ]

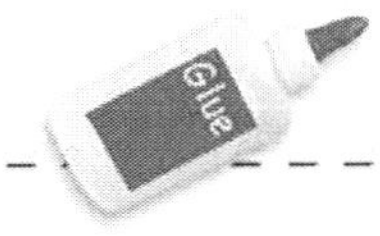

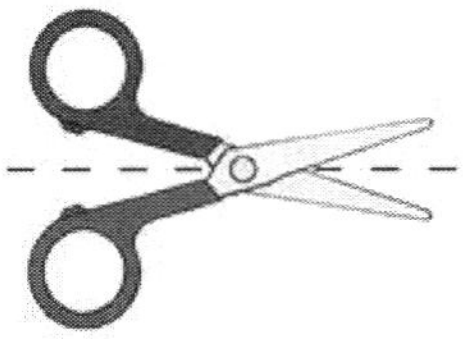

Cut out the punctuation below and glue them in the correct boxes above.

[.] [?] [!] [?] [?] [!]

8.2 - Letter Ff   128

My name is _____.

Trace:

Color:

Write this sentence below: Look and jump a little.

Cut out the letters below. Glue them in these boxes to make your sight words.

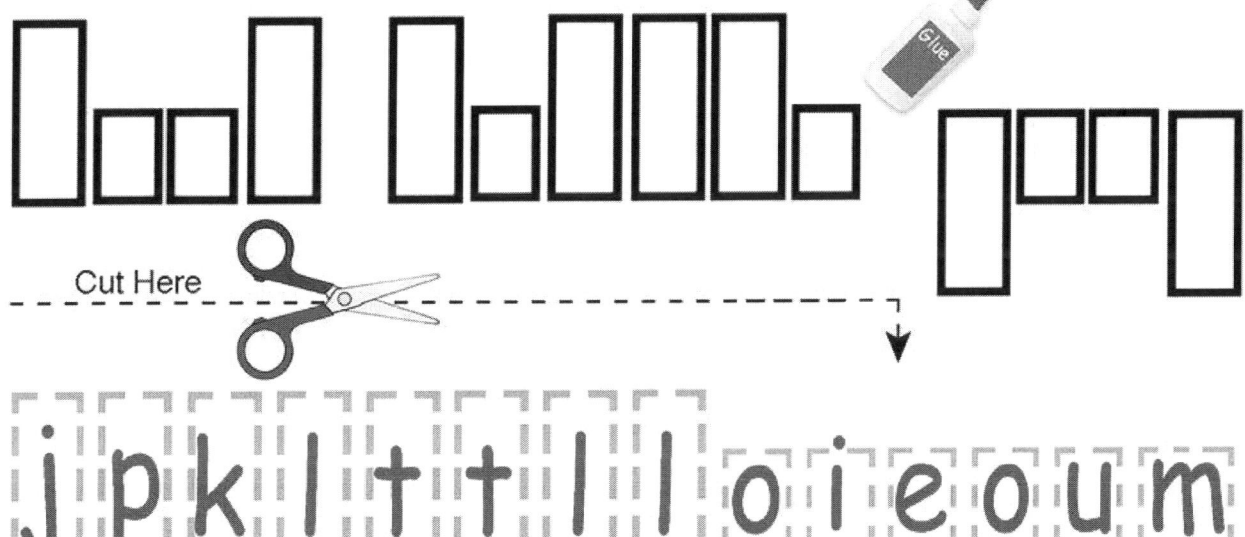

Cut Here

8.3 - Letter Ff

My name is _____.

Making Sentence Cubes

Directions:

1) Cut out the cubes on the following three pages.

2) Fold the tabs in and ask an adult to help you fold and glue each cube.

3) Roll the cubes. Read the one that starts with the uppercase letter first, then read the cube that starts with a lowercase letter, then read the third cube that ends with punctuation. Repeat at least 5 times.

4) Choose one of the complete sentences you roll that makes sense. Write it below:

8.4 - Letter Ff

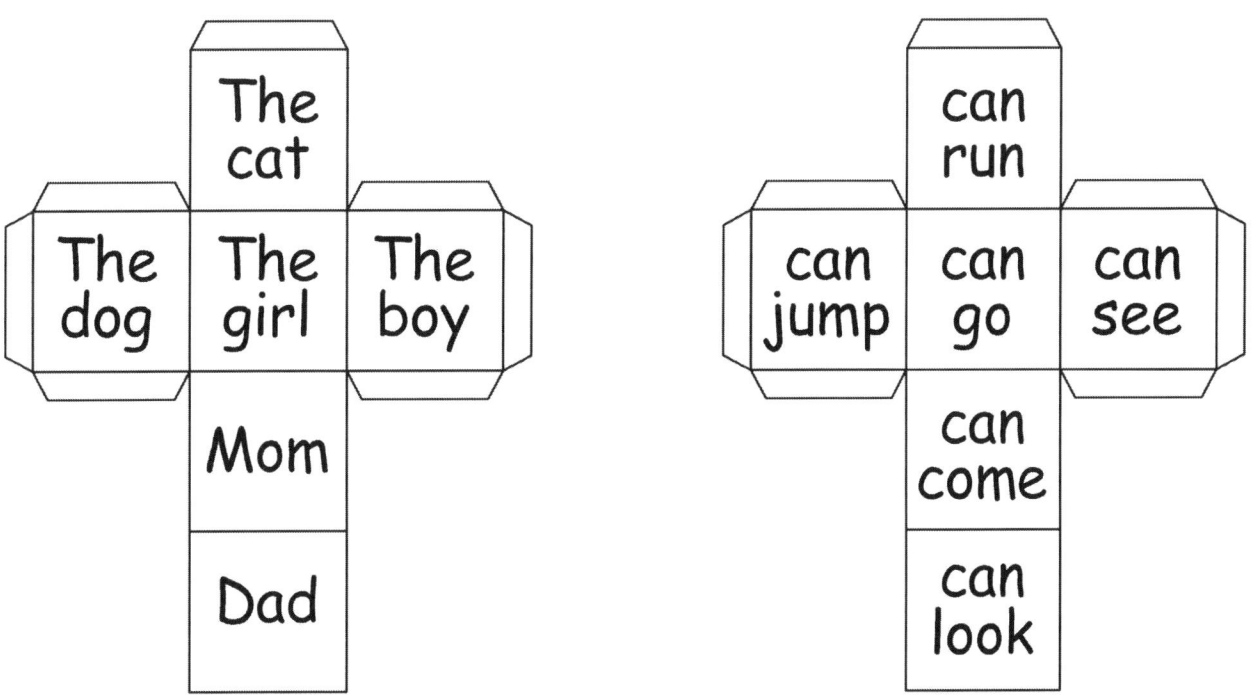

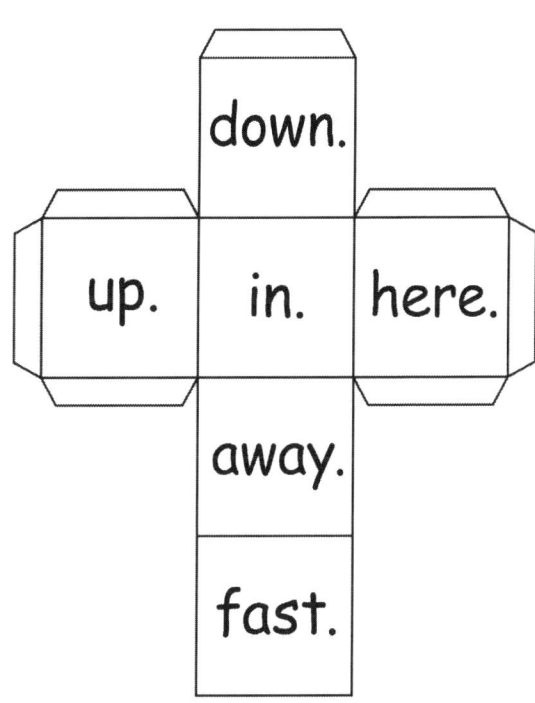

Continue on next page.

8.4 - Letter Ff

My name is _____ .   **Sorting**

Directions: Cut out the items on the following page and sort them. Glue them in the correct box on this page.

Continue on the next page.

9.2 - Letter Dd

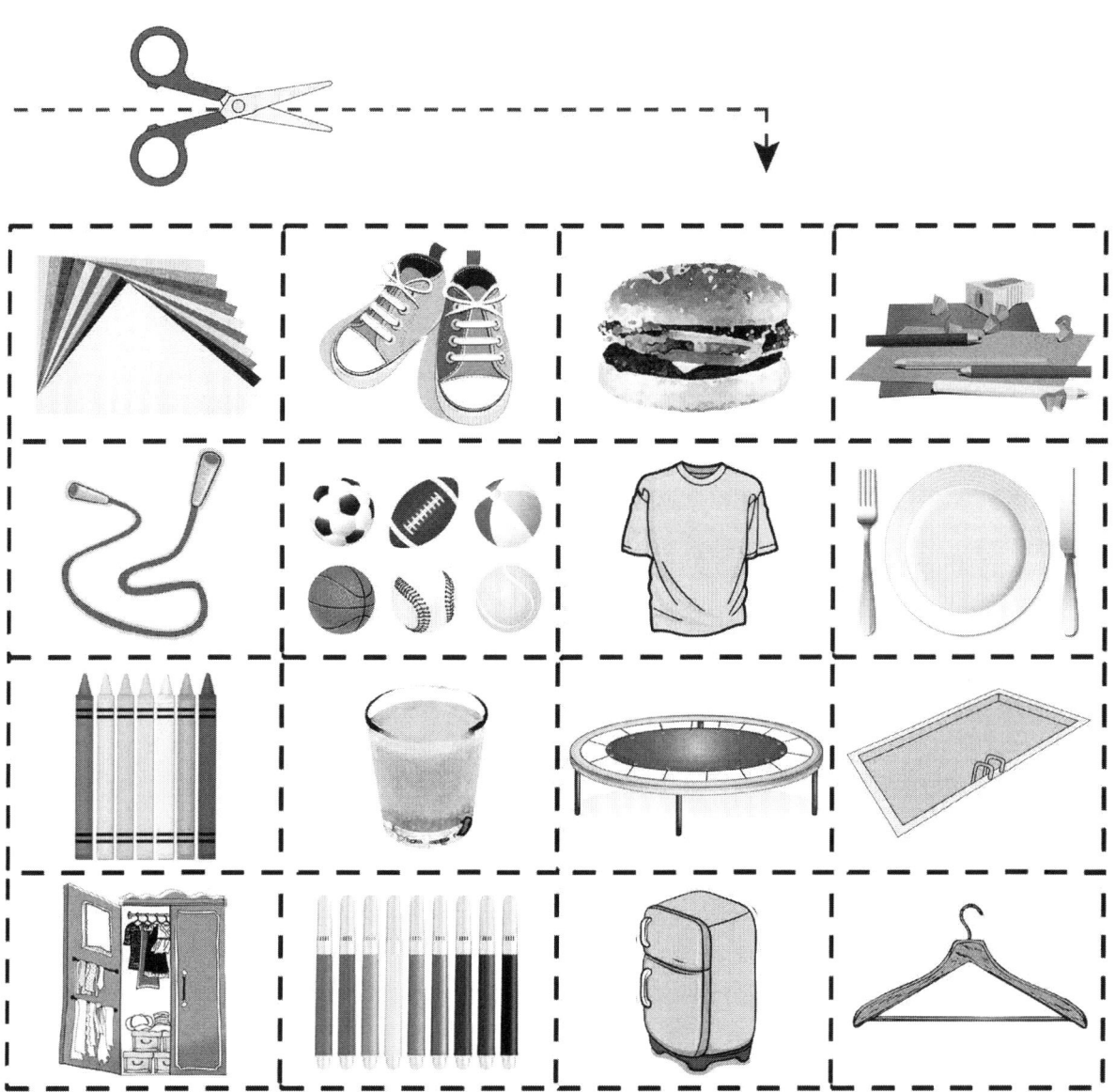

9.2 - Letter Dd

My name is _____.

Trace:

make me away

Color:

away make me

Write this sentence below: It can make me go away.

Cut out the letters below. Glue them in these boxes to make your sight words.

Cut Here

e m a w a w a a k e m y

9.3 - Letter Dd

Antonyms

Cut out the pictures and pair the **antonyms** (opposites) together.

Continue on the next page.

My name is _____ .

Glue the **antonyms** of (opposites) side by side.

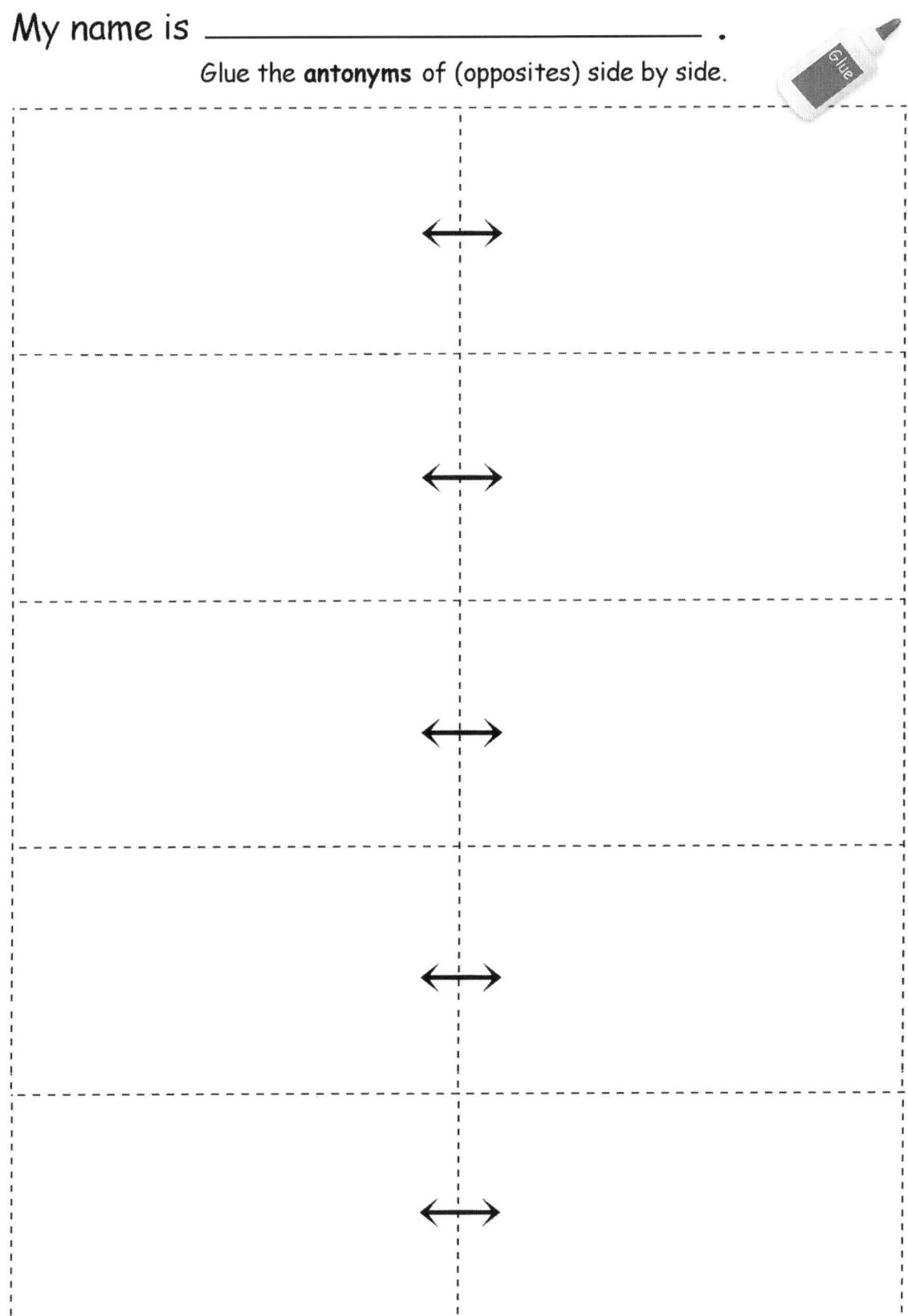

10.2 - Letter Gg

 My name is _____ .

Trace:

Color:

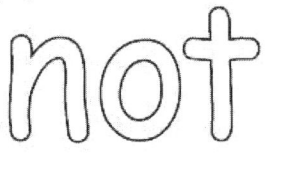 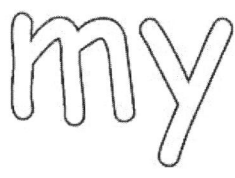 

Write this sentence below: It is not my little one.

 Cut out the letters below. Glue them in these boxes to make your sight words.

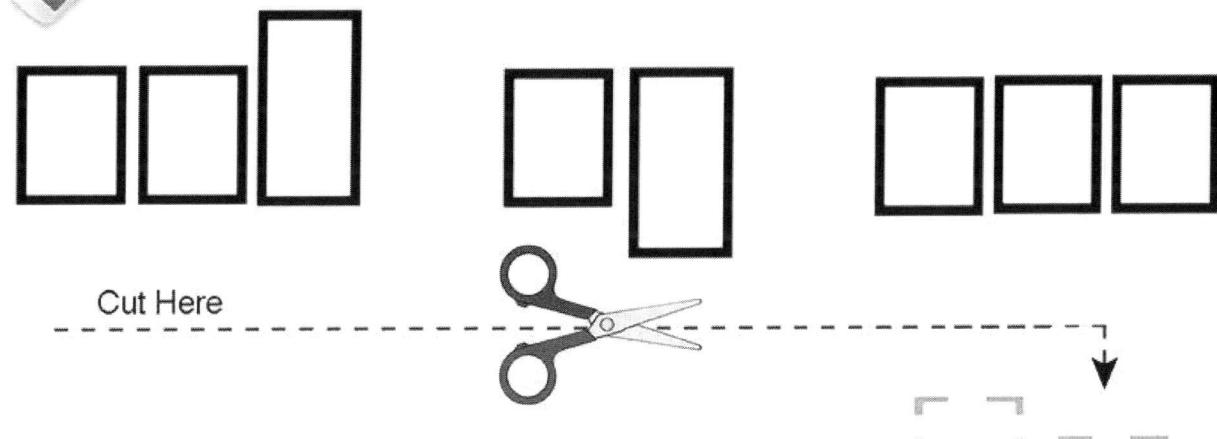

Cut Here

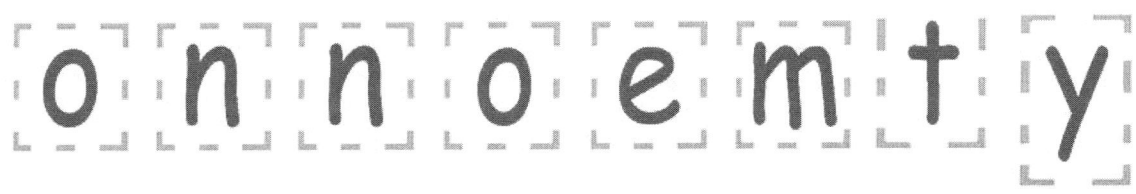

10.3 - Letter Gg

Capitalizing I

Name _____.

Glue the sentences with the capital **I** under the **Correct** column.

Glue the sentences with the lowercase letter **i** under **Not Correct** column.

Correct	Not Correct

Cut Here

i can play with you.	I can look for it.
Can I find it?	Can you and i find it?
i can jump!	I see a big can.

Continue on following page.

11.2 - Letter Ii

My name is _____.

First Letter Family

Read the sentences. Cut out the correct word and glue it on the line.

☐ play with me.		☐ can go with you.	
☐ iguana is big.		☐ I go in the igloo?	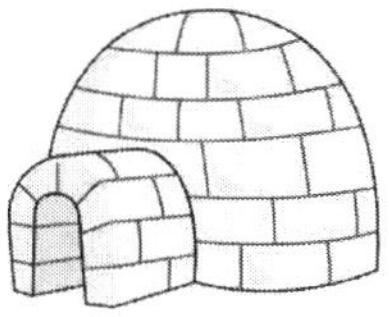
☐ is a little one!		☐ the insect blue?	

Cut out these words and glue them in the correct boxes above.

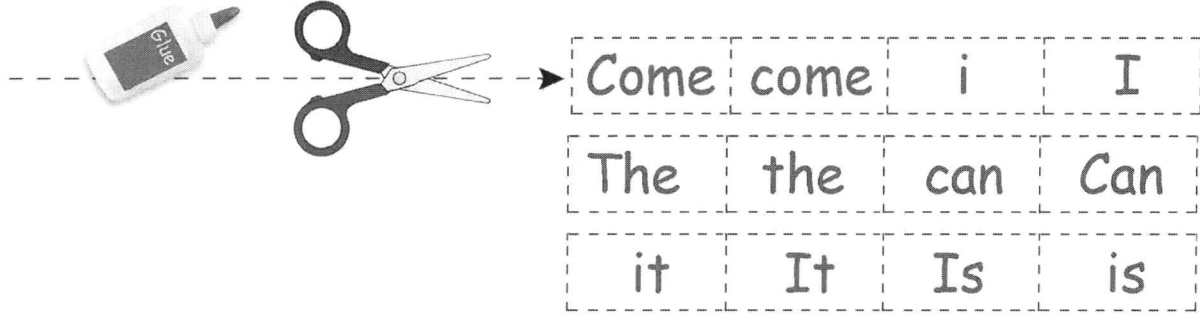

Come	come	i	I
The	the	can	Can
it	It	Is	is

11.2 - Letter Ii   150

My name is _____.

Trace:

play with you

Color:

with you play

Write this sentence below: I can play with you.

Cut out the letters below. Glue them in these boxes to make your sight words.

Cut Here

y i a l o w t p u h y

Name _____

Come Play with Me

How can we expand sentences?

1. We can add describing words (adjectives). Cut out the adjectives and glue them into the blue boxes.

Come in the igloo with me, [ ] insect and [ ] iguana.

2. We can add more information. Measure the length of the iguana and glue it into the blue box.

I look at the iguana and see it is [ ].

little   big

ten inches.

words

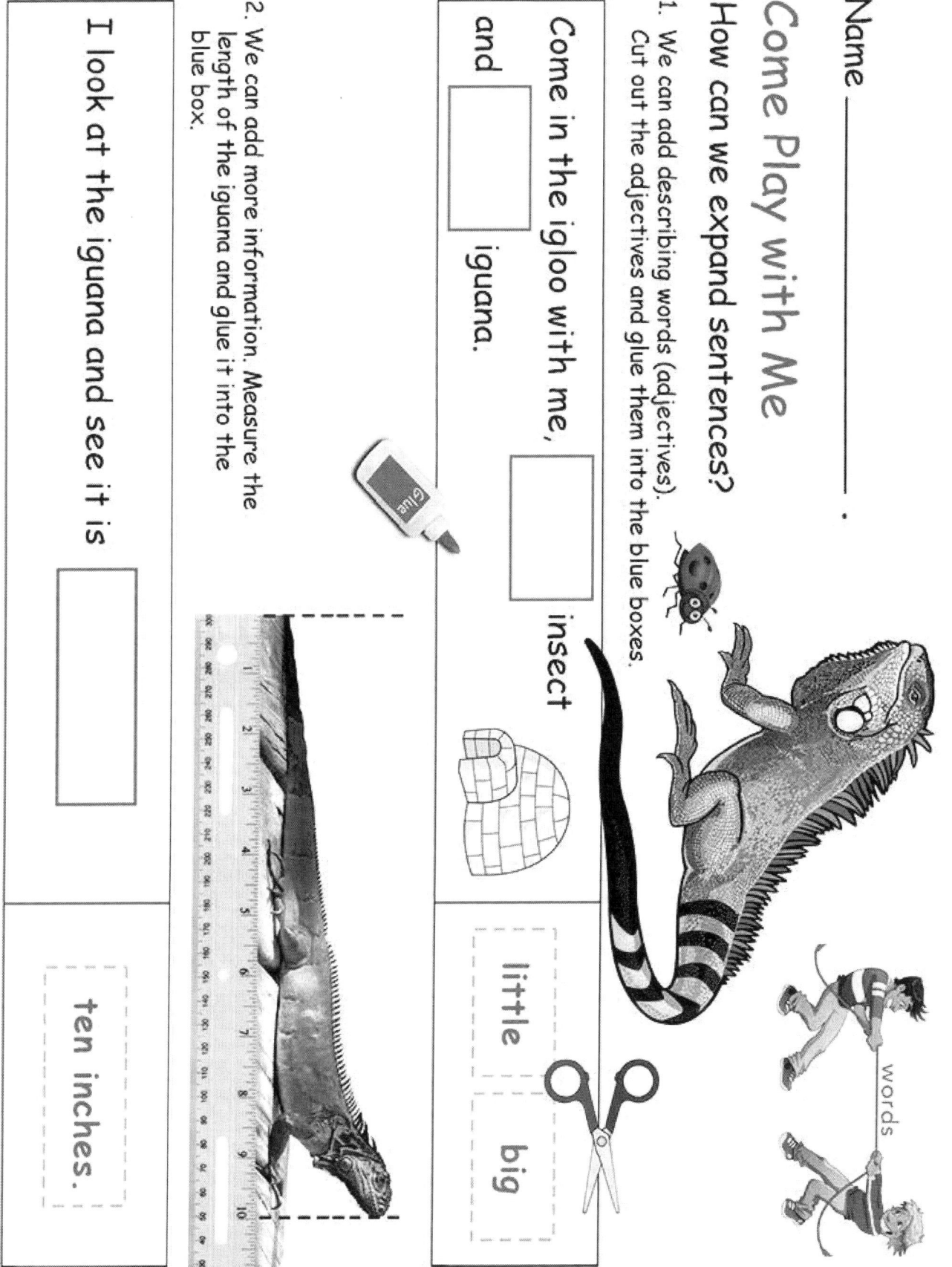

11.5 - Letter Ii

Sight Word Leaves

Cut them out!

Print the pages of leaves on the following pages. Write one sight word on each leaf. Cut around the leaves. Leap as you read each word.

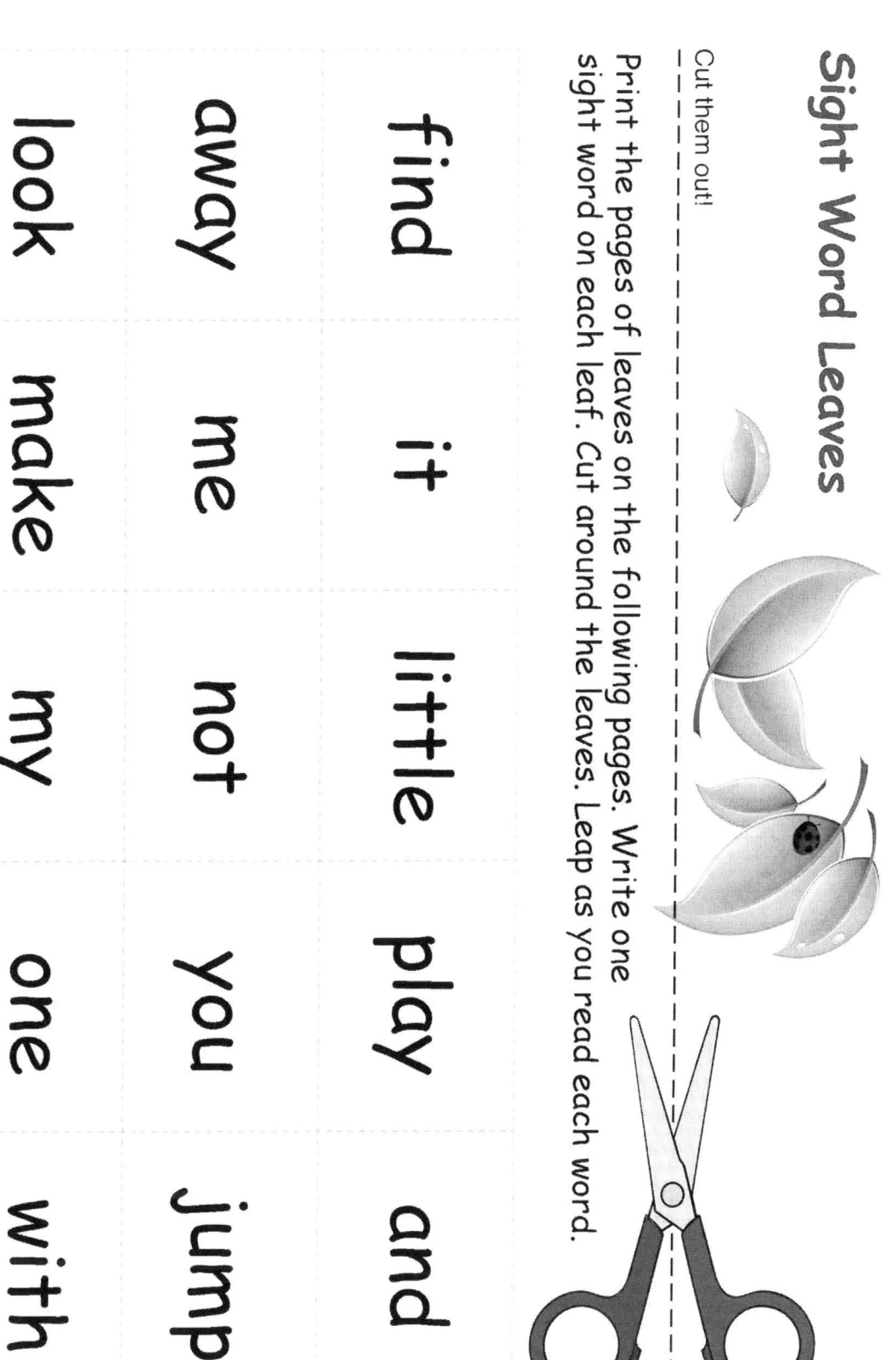

find	it	little	play	and
away	me	not	you	jump
look	make	my	one	with

Continue on following pages.

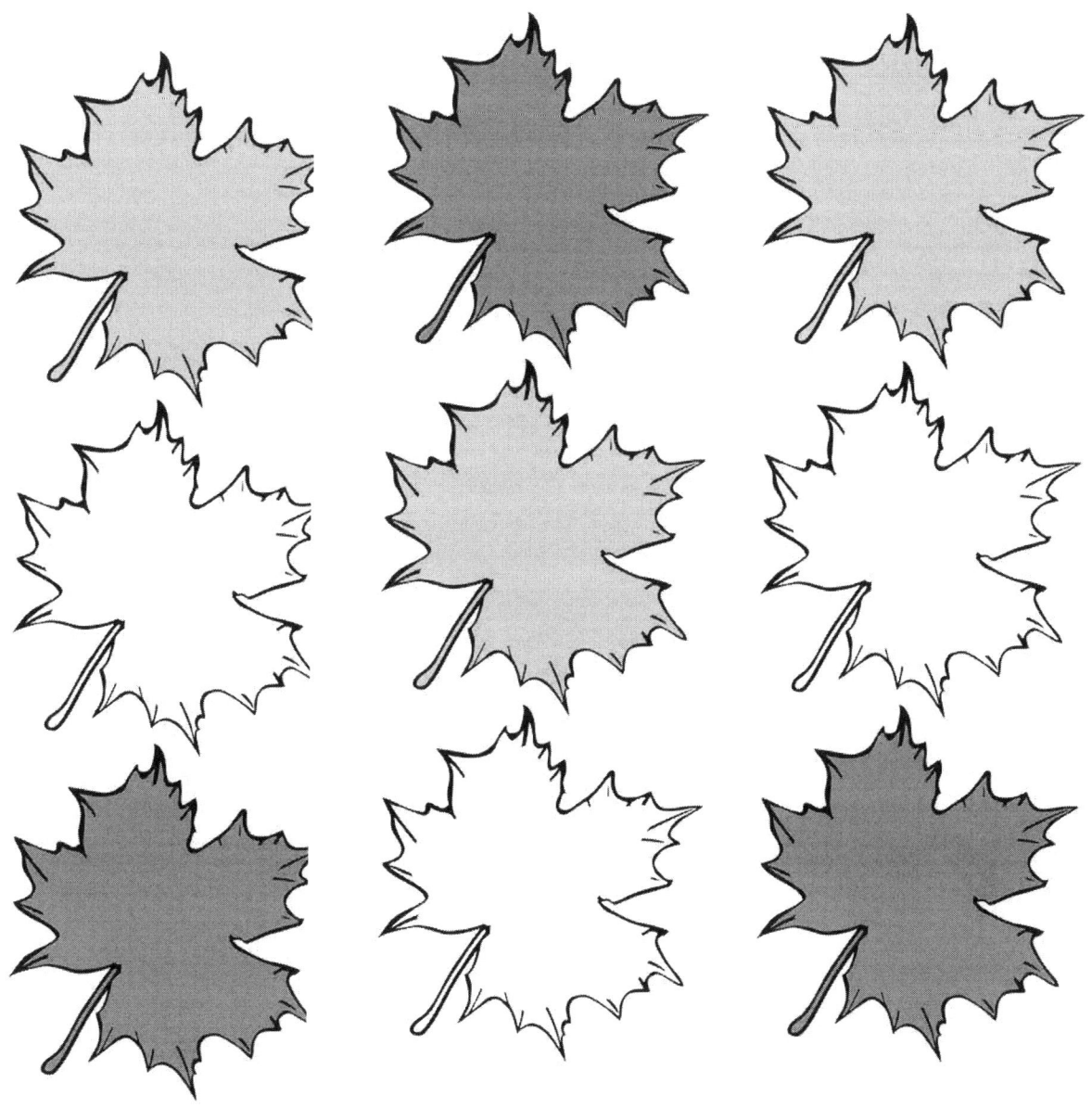

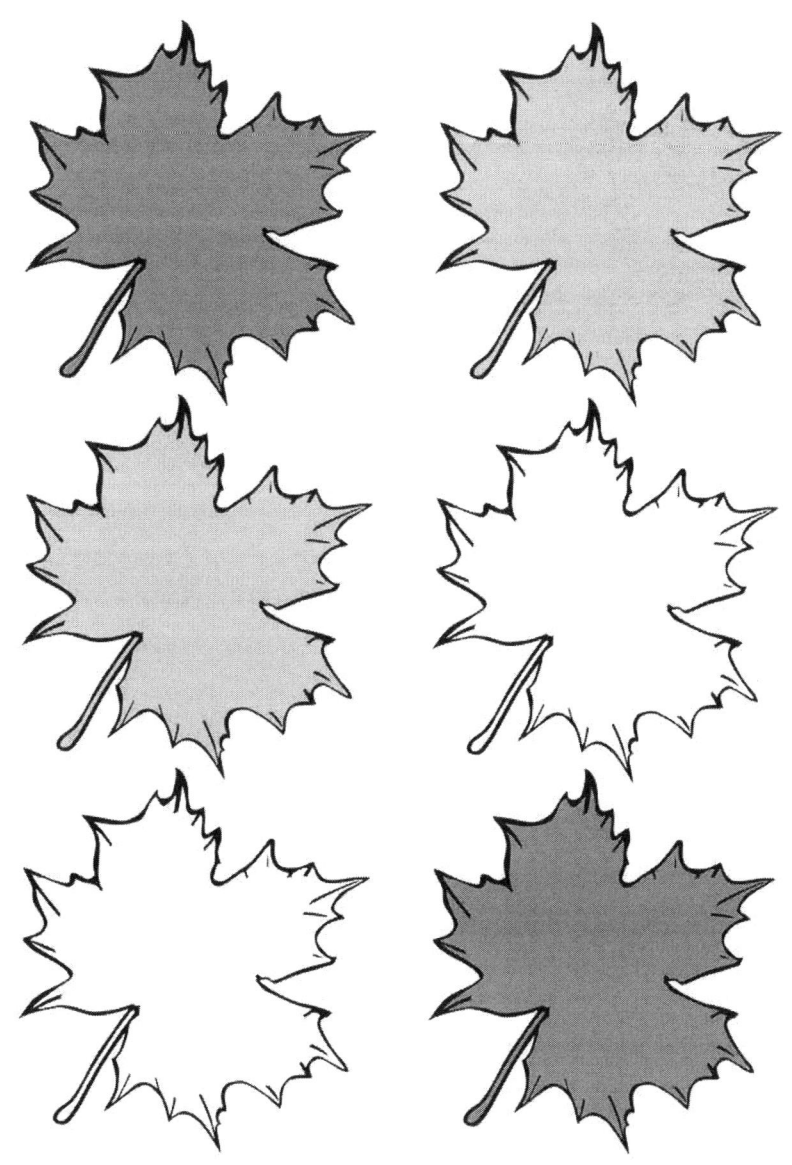

My name is _____.

Trace:

Color:

Write this sentence below: I can go up to three.

_____

_____

 Cut out the letters below. Glue them in these boxes to make your sight words.

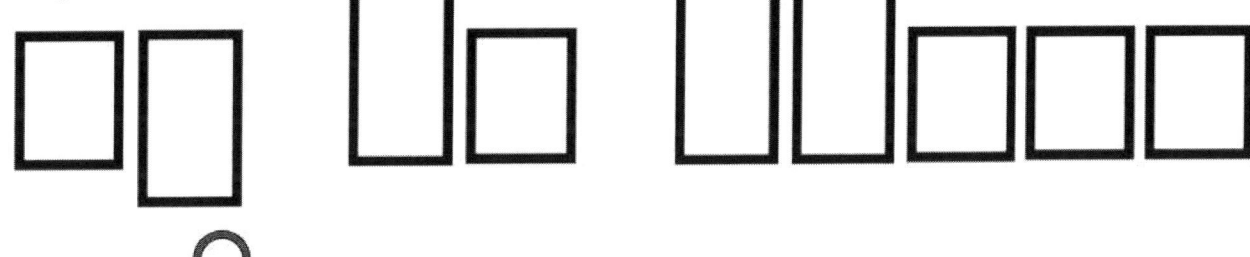

Cut Here

My name is _____ .

My Cat is Three
Words that start with C:

1. Cut out the **c** words at the bottom of the page.
2. Read the story on the second page.
3. Glue the correct words on the blanks to complete the story.

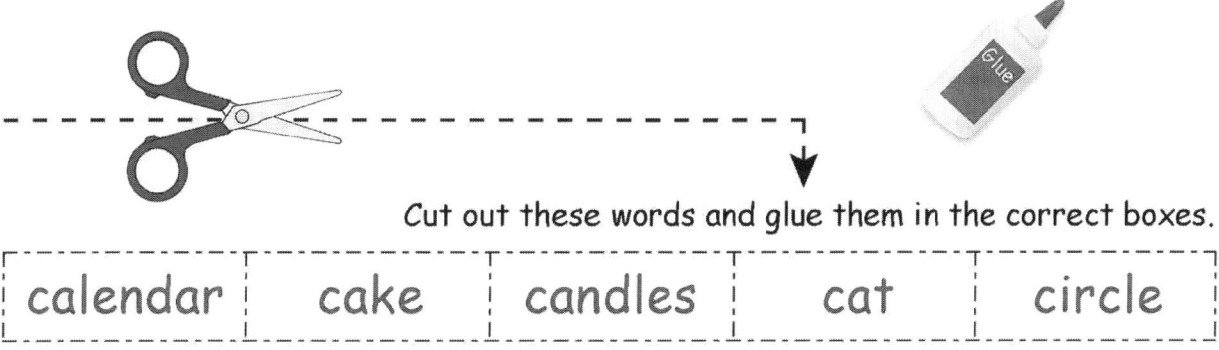

Cut out these words and glue them in the correct boxes.

| calendar | cake | candles | cat | circle |

Continue on next page.

13.4 - Letter Cc

I see a . I can make a ◯. It is

the big one! My 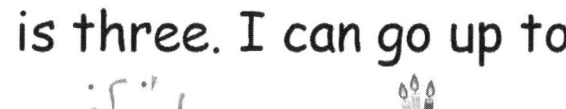 is three. I can go up to

three. One, two, three. I can make a .

I can go up to three. One, two, three.
Come here, cat. It is the big one for you! Here you go. Can you see the three? I can go up to three One, two, three.

Here you go. Can you see three ? I can go

up to three. One, two, three. Happy Birthday, Cat!

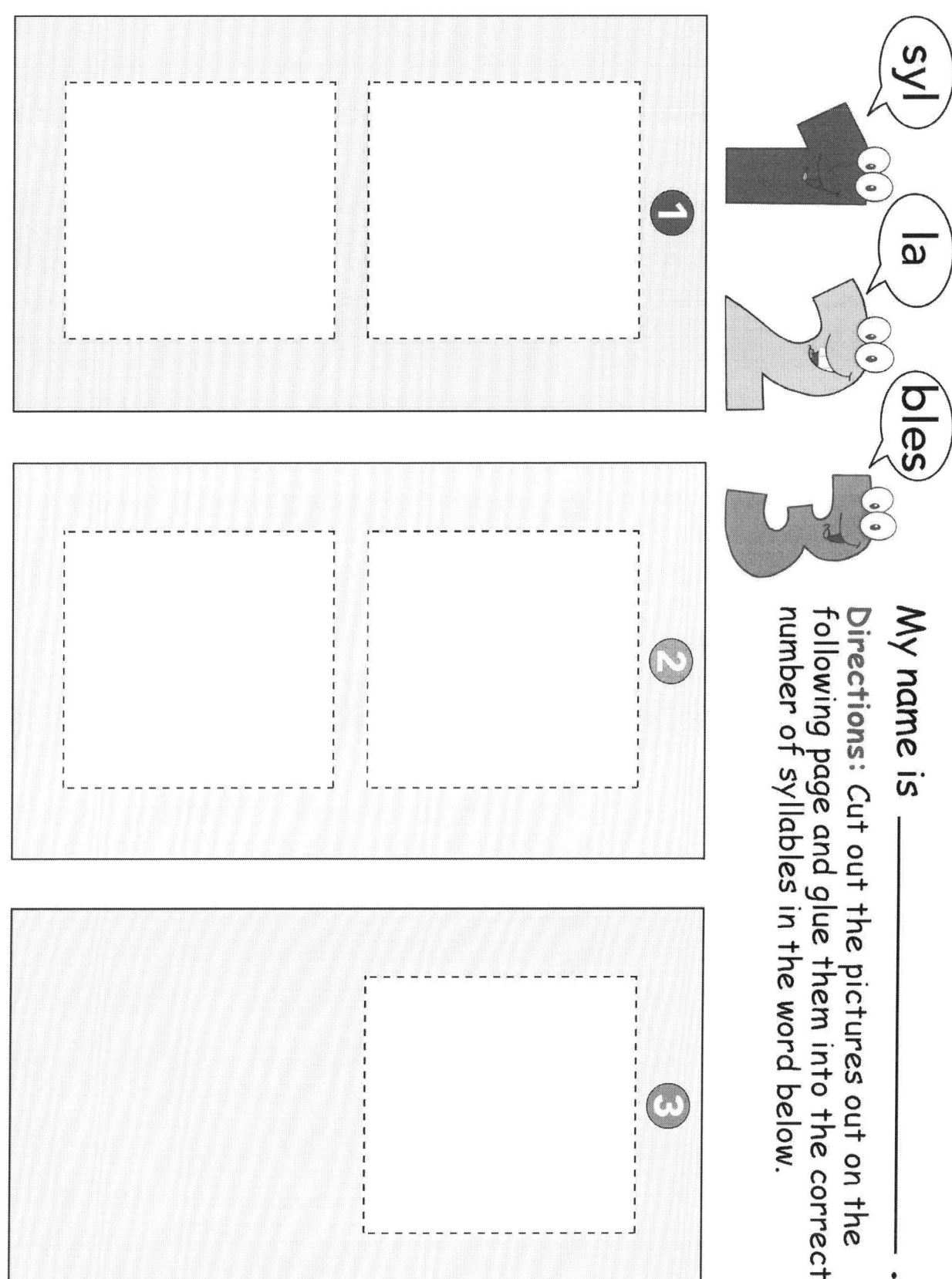

My name is _____.

Directions: Cut out the pictures out on the following page and glue them into the correct number of syllables in the word below.

Continue on following page.

14.2 - Letter Pp

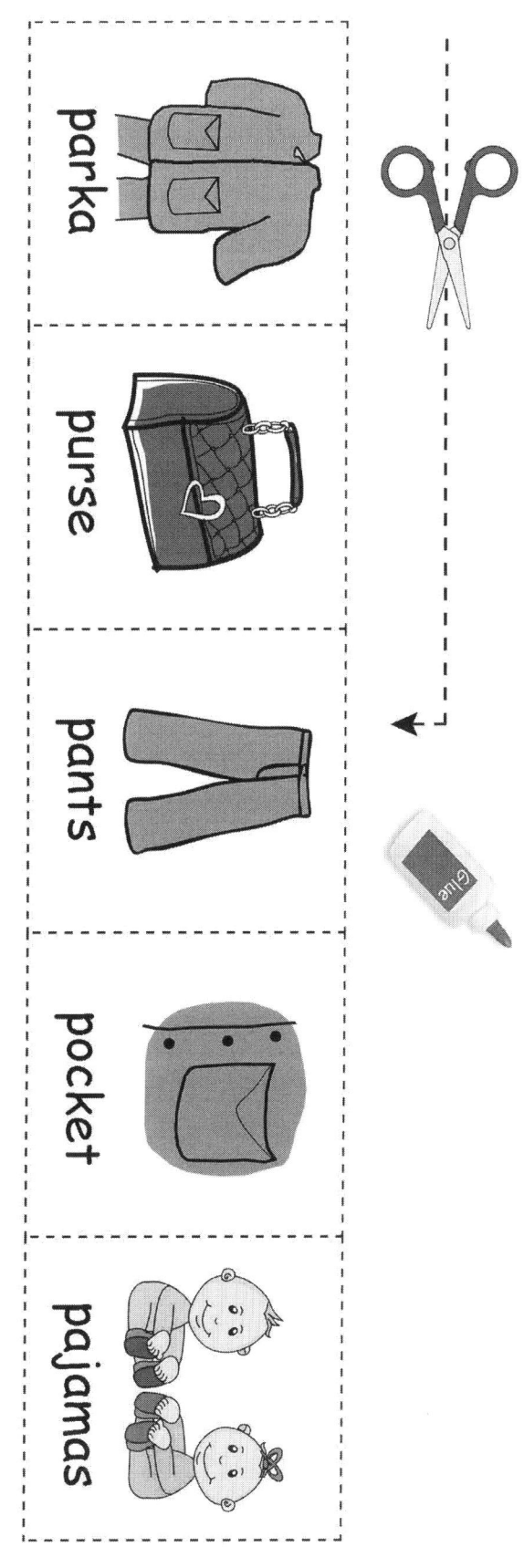

14.2 - Letter Pp

My name is _____.

Trace:

we two where

Color:

where two we

Write this sentence below: Where can we find two?

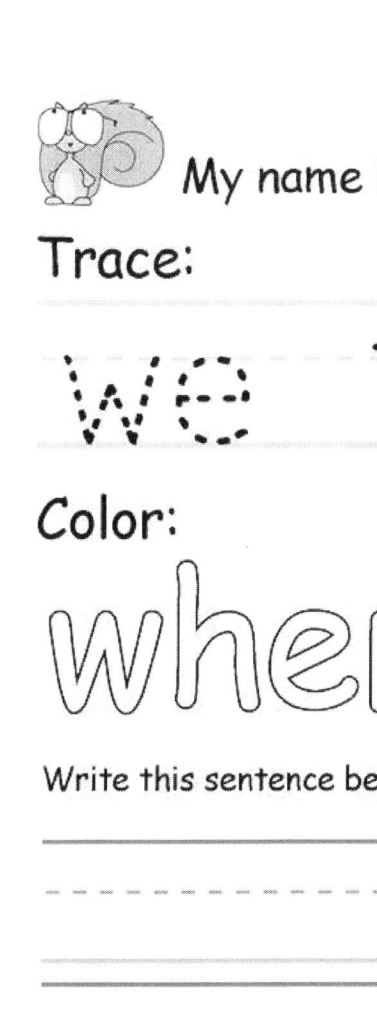

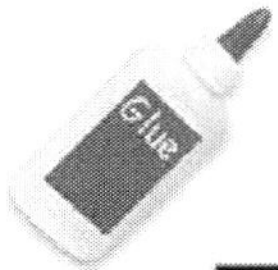

Cut out the letters below. Glue them in these boxes to make your sight words.

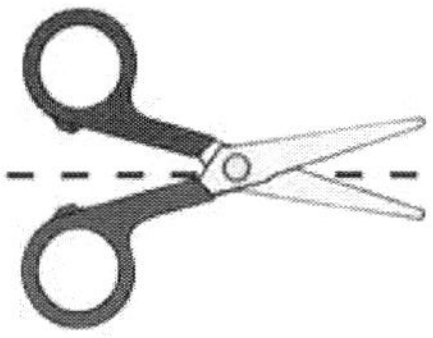

☐ ☐☐☐ ☐☐ ☐☐☐

Cut Here

w o e h e w t e w r

Character Passport

Directions:

1. Choose one character from any of your weekly or Independent Reading stories.
2. Create a passport page for your character by drawing and filling out the passport pages.
3. Cut the passport pages in half and cut this page in half and staple the passport cover on top of the two character passport pages to make a passport.

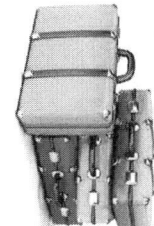

- - - - - - - - - - - - - Cut Here - - - - - - - - - - - - -

Character Passport

Issued by: _____

(Student name)

14.4 - Letter Pp

Character Passport

Character's Photo

Name: _____
(Name of character)

From: _____
(Title (name) of story)

Mark one:
- ☐ Boy ☐ Mom ☐ Animal
- ☐ Girl ☐ Dad

Passport Stamp

About Me:
(Setting of the story)

APPROVED

_____
_____
_____
Character Fact

14.4 - Letter Pp

Word Family Cards

1. Print the first two pages on cardstock and the third page on regular paper.
2. Cut out the word family cards and cut out small squares to make windows.
3. Cut out the letter strips.
4. Put each letter strip behind its corresponding word family card. Slowly pull the letter strip through and sound out the words.
5. Write each word you make on the third page to turn into your teacher.

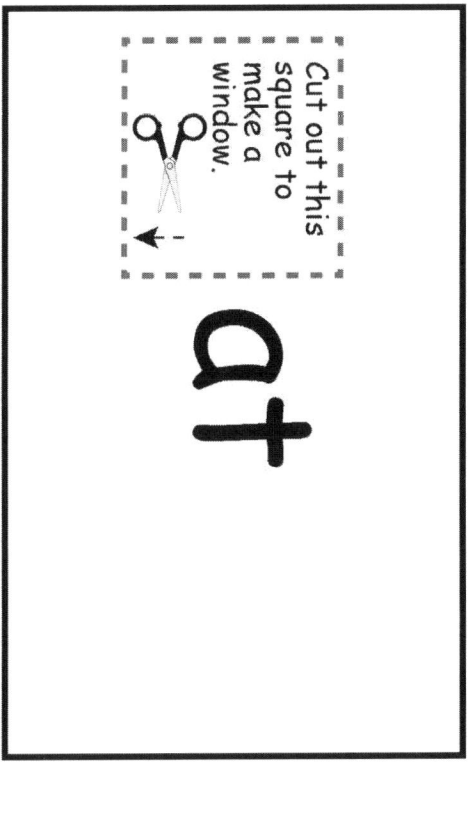

at

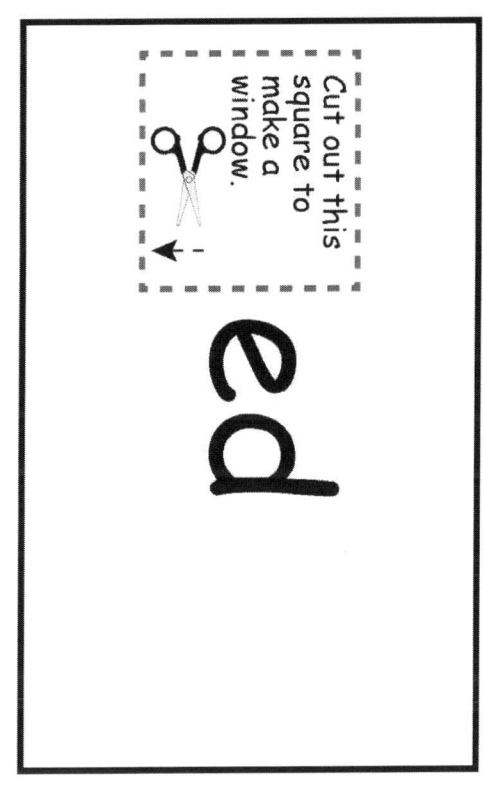

ed

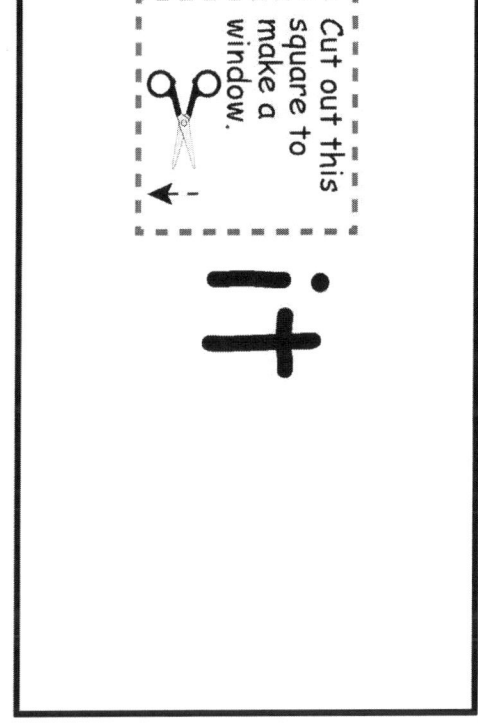

it

Continue on the next page.

| T | r | l | f | b | ed |

| c | h | s | p | m | at |

| k | h | s | f | b | it |

Continue on the next page.

Word Families

at Family
1. _____
2. _____
3. _____
4. _____
5. _____
6. _____

ed Family
1. _____
2. _____
3. _____
4. _____
5. _____

it Family
1. _____
2. _____
3. _____
4. _____
5. _____

My name is _____.

Trace:

red yellow am

Color:

am yellow red

Write this sentence below: I am yellow and red.

Cut out the letters below. Glue them in these boxes to make your sight words.

Cut Here

w o e l a r l y m d e

My name is _____.

Trace:

eat did ate

Color:

did eat ate

Write this sentence below: I can eat. Yes, I ate oranges.

_____

_____

Cut out the letters below. Glue them in these boxes to make your sight words.

☐☐☐   ☐☐☐   ☐☐☐

Cut Here

d e t a t i e d a

16.3 - Letter Oo

Types of Texts Cards

Cut out the cards and glue them on the second page under the correct type of text.

Cut Here

 "Little Red Riding Hood"	"Farm Animals"
"Jack and Jill" 	"Humpty Dumpty"
"Goldilocks and the Three Bears" 	"Weather" 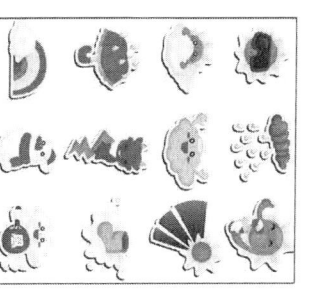

Continue on the next page.

17.2 - Letter Hh

My name is _____.

Types of Texts:

*Glue the **Types of Texts** cards under the correct category.*

Poems and Nursery Rhymes:	Storybooks:	Nonfiction:

 My name is _____.

Trace:

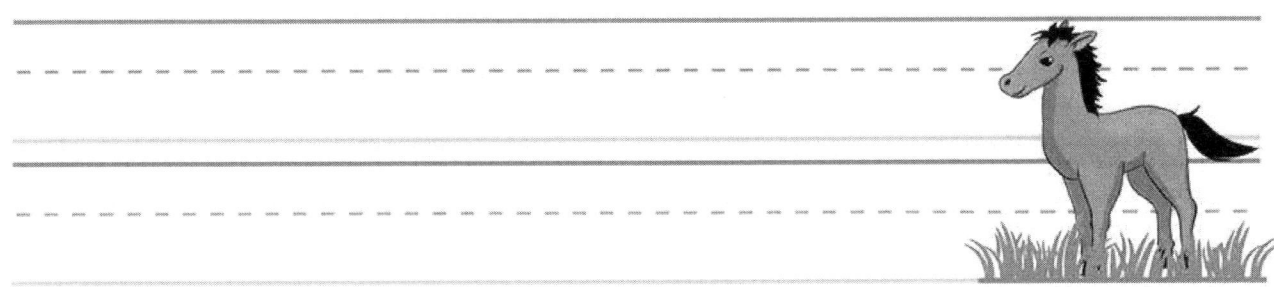

Write this sentence below: Help me find the brown and black horse.

 Cut out the letters below. Glue them in these boxes to make your sight words.

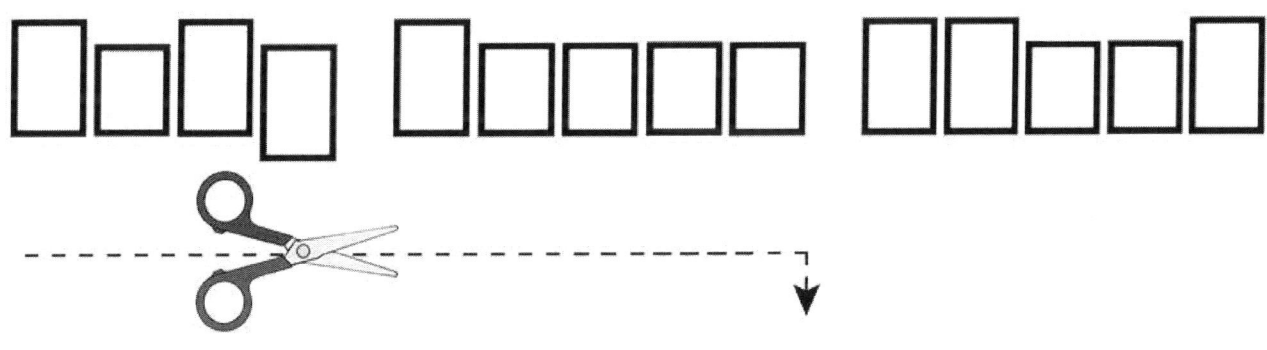

17.3 - Letter Hh

What's the Main Idea?

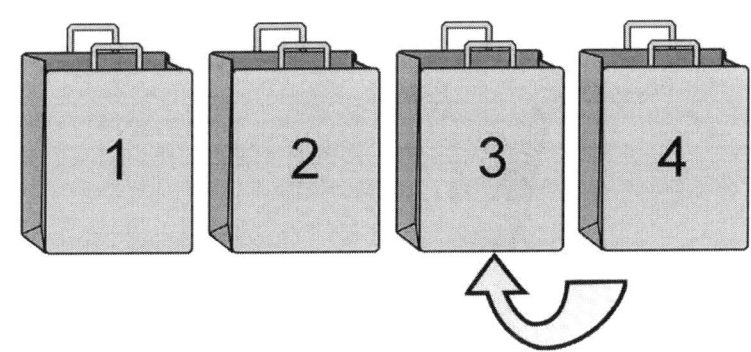

Adult:

1) Write numbers 1-4 on the front of each paper bag.

2) Write one main idea on the bottom of each paper bag.
   1. Kangaroos
   2. How important friends are.
   3. Where you live.
   4. The Titanic

Student:

1) Cut out the cards on the following pages and place them in the corresponding bag.

2) Read the underlined/yellow words and ask an adult to read the rest of the clue. If there is an ear in front of the word, it is not a sight word but it is a word you can sound out.

3) State the main idea. **What were the clues in the bag mainly about?** Then look at the bottom of the bag to check your answer.

Continue on the next page.

Bag #1

A baby kangaroo is called a joey.	A joey stays in its mother's pouch until it is 8 months old.
When the red kangaroo is full grown, it is 6 feet tall.	A red kangaroo can jump 30 feet with each leap.

Bag #2

Friends can help you if something is hard.	Friends can make you feel better when you feel  sad.
You can play and have fun with your friends.	I know how important it is to have friends.

Continue on the next page.

Bag #3

Where do you live?	Do you live in a busy city with tall buildings?
Do you live in the country with 👂 lots of 👂 land?	Do you live in a suburb with houses and shops?

Bag #4

The Titanic sunk.	The Titanic was a gigantic ship.
There were over 2,000 people 👂 on the ship.	The Titanic 👂 hit 👂 an iceberg.

Continue on the next page.

Name _____.

What's the Main Idea?

Idea

1 The clues in this bag were mainly about...

2 The clues in this bag were mainly about...

3 The clues in this bag were mainly about...

4 The clues in this bag were mainly about...

18.4 - Letter Vv

Weekly Sight Words

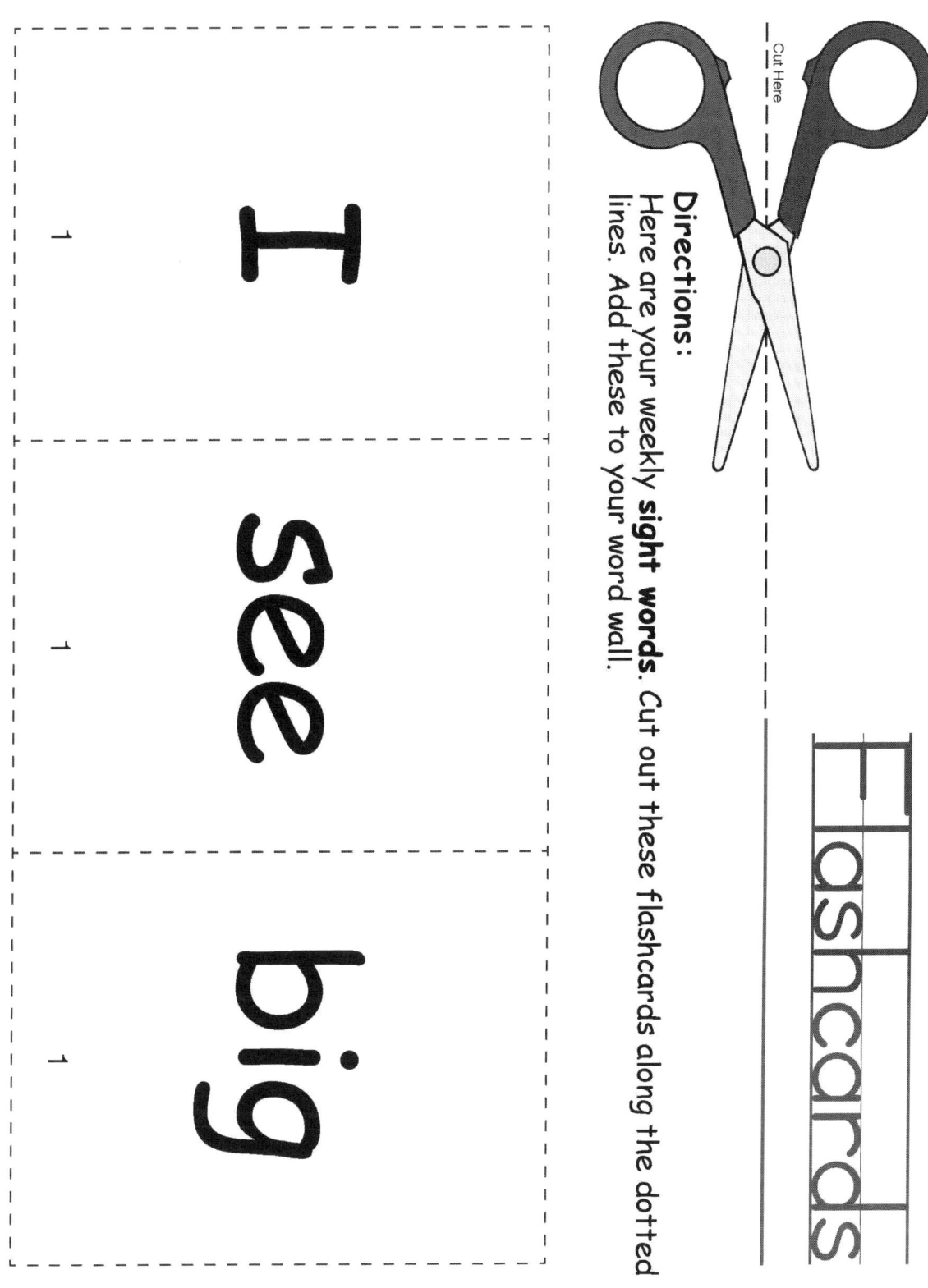

Directions:
Here are your weekly **sight words**. Cut out these flashcards along the dotted lines. Add these to your word wall.

Flashcards

I

see

big

1.1 - Letter Aa

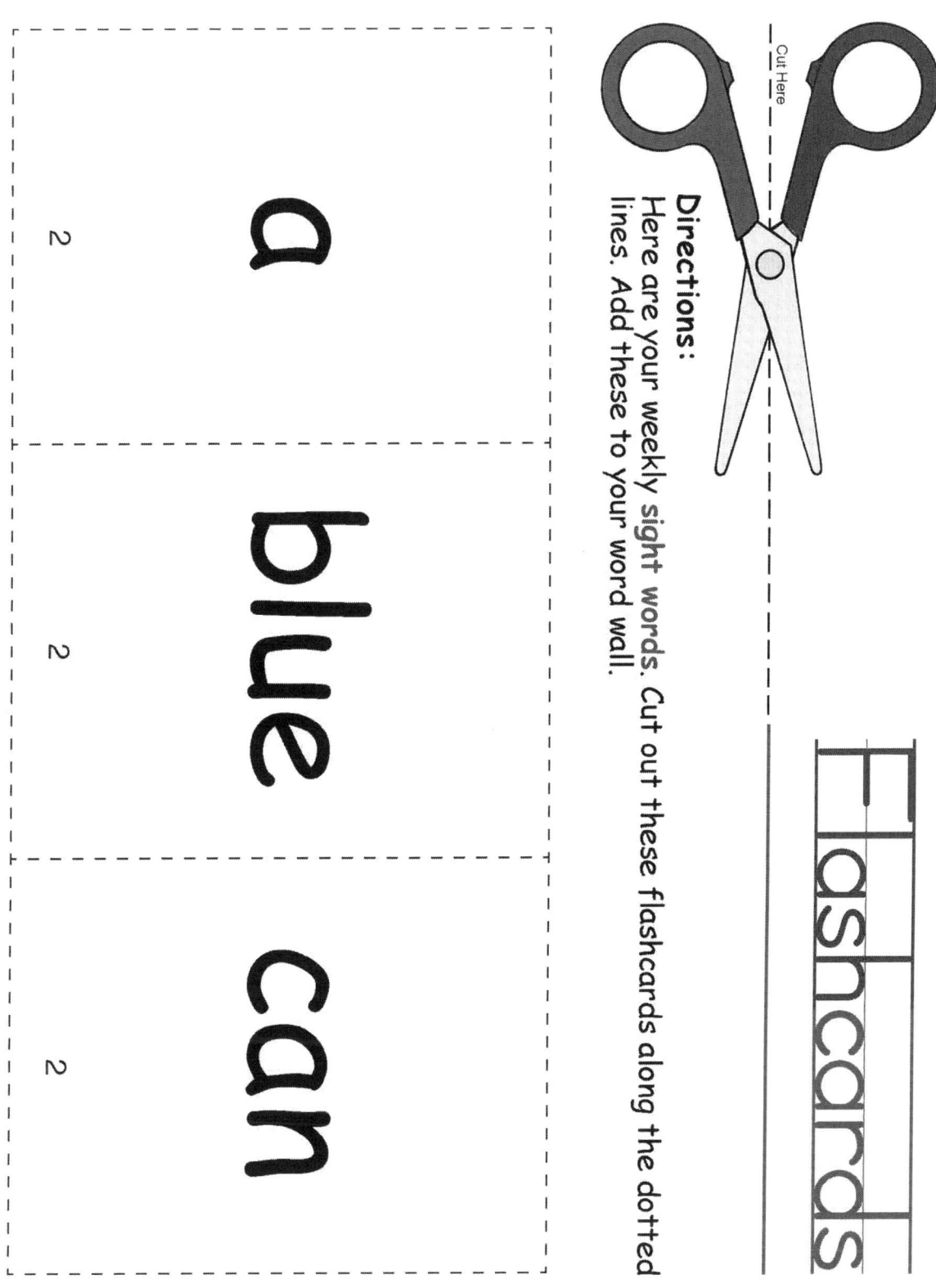

Directions:
Here are your weekly sight words. Cut out these flashcards along the dotted lines. Add these to your word wall.

Flashcards

a	blue	can
2	2	2

2.1 - Letter Bb

Directions:
Here are your weekly sight words. Cut out these flashcards along the dotted lines. Add these to your word wall.

Flashcards

the	said	in
3	3	3

3.1 - Letter Tt

Directions:
Here are your weekly sight words. Cut out these flashcards along the dotted lines. Add these to your word wall.

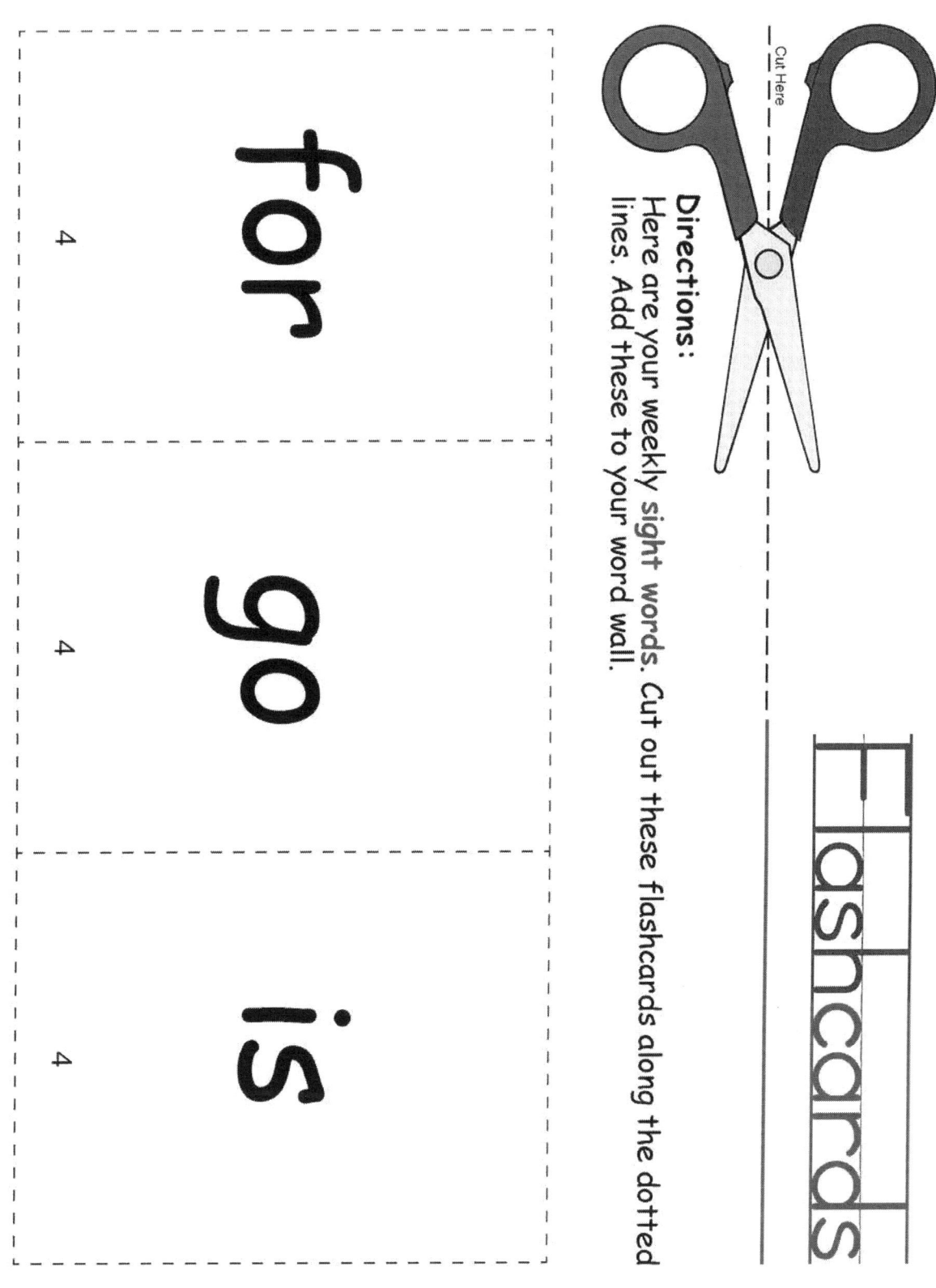

for

go

is

4.1 - Letter Mm

Flashcards

Directions:
Here are your weekly sight words. Cut out these flashcards along the dotted lines. Add these to your word wall.

come	down	here
5	5	5

5.1 - Letter Ss

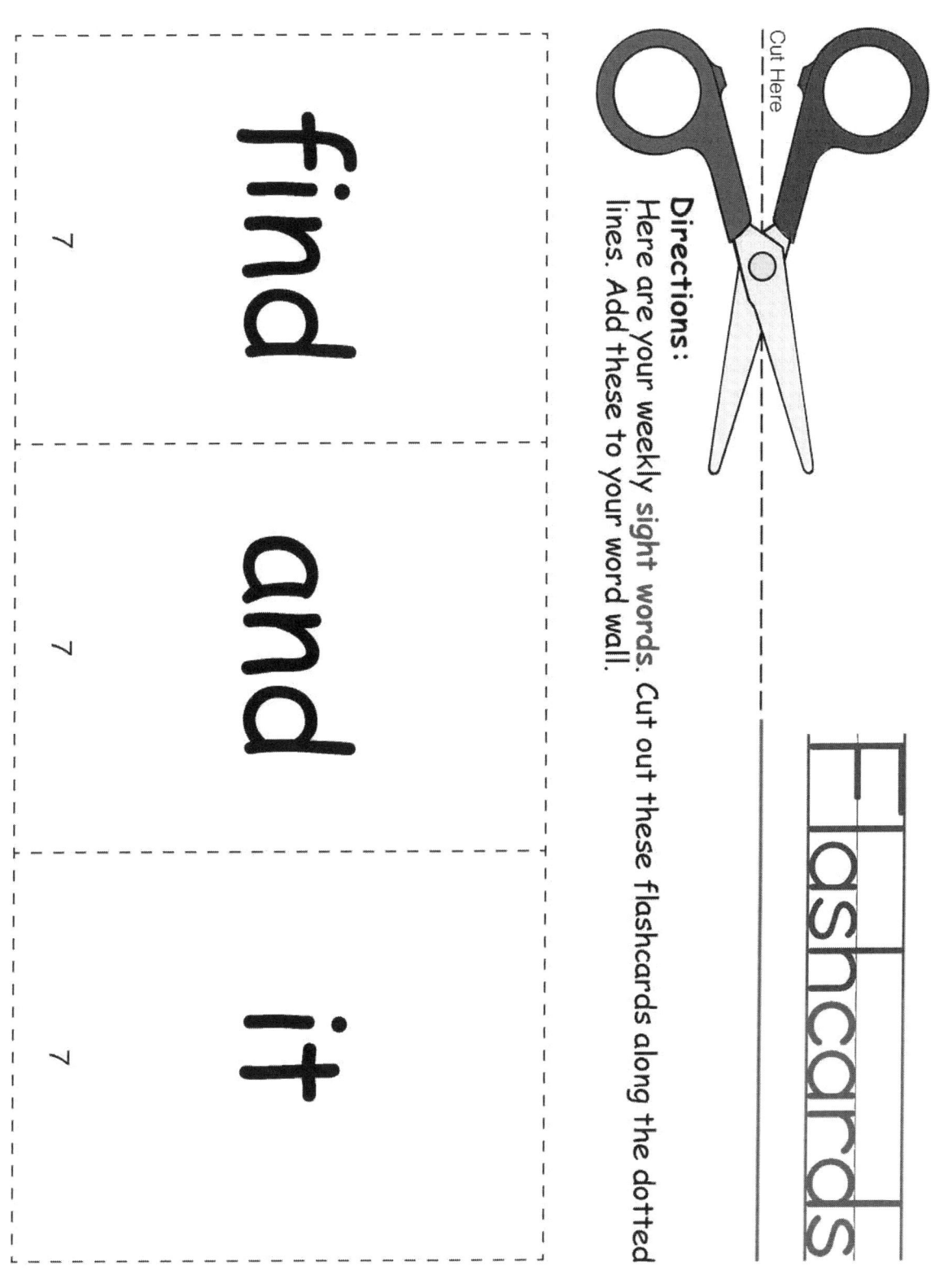

Directions:
Here are your weekly sight words. Cut out these flashcards along the dotted lines. Add these to your word wall.

Flashcards

| find | and | it |

7.1 - Letter Ee

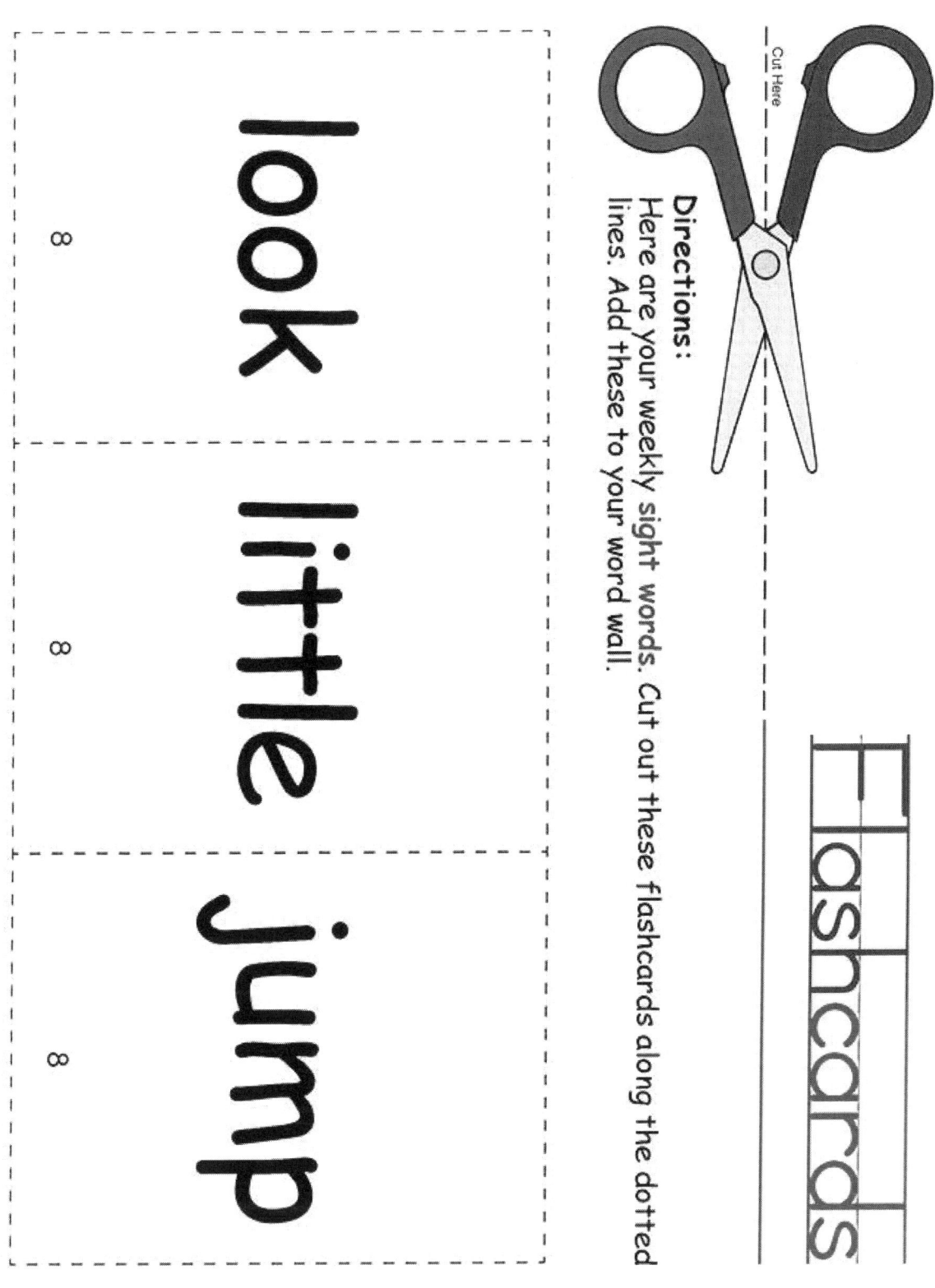

Directions:
Here are your weekly sight words. Cut out these flashcards along the dotted lines. Add these to your word wall.

Flashcards

look

little

jump

8.1 - Letter Ff

Flashcards

Directions:
Here are your weekly sight words. Cut out these flashcards along the dotted lines. Add these to your word wall.

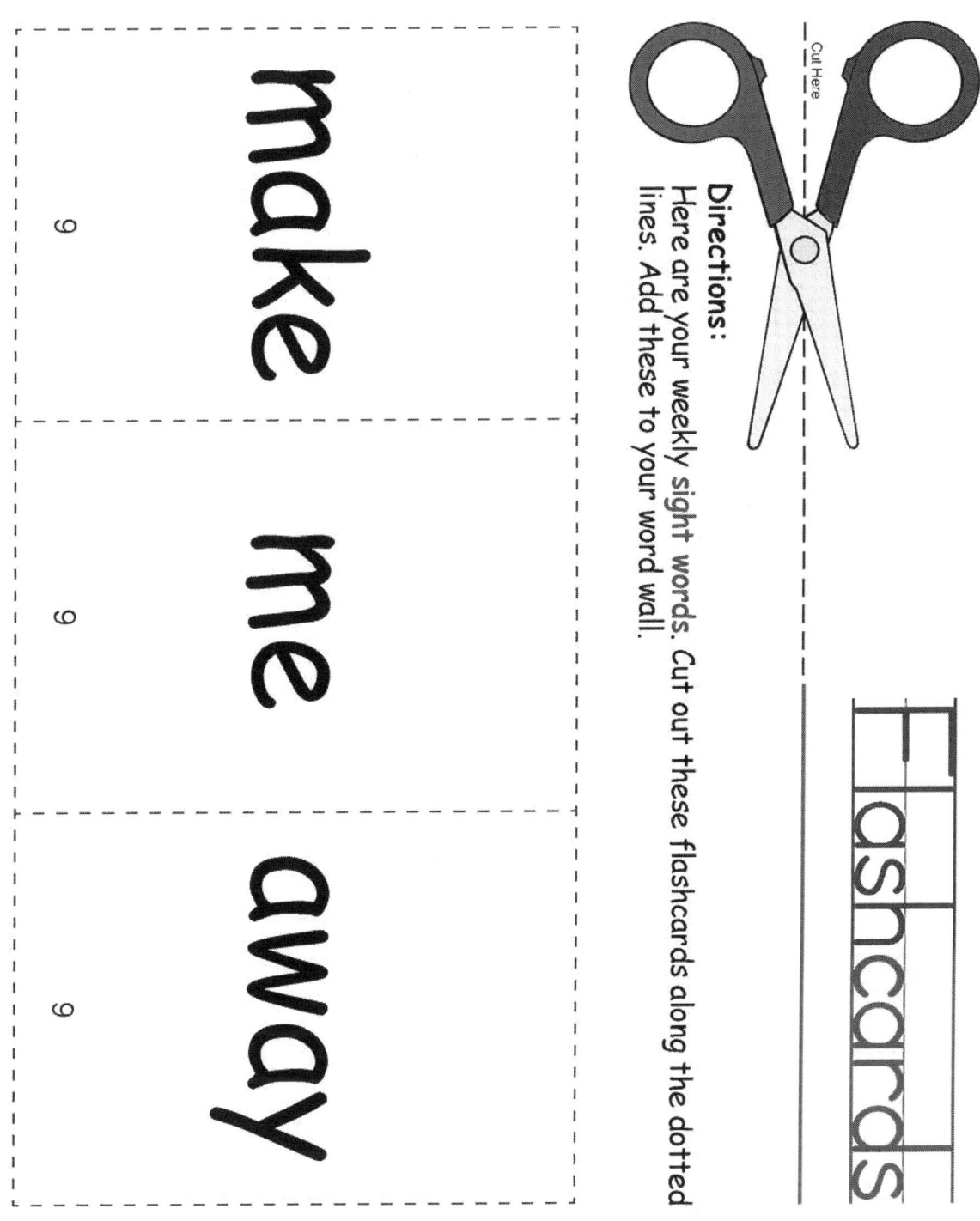

- make
- me
- away

9.1 - Letter Dd

Directions:
Here are your weekly sight words. Cut out these flashcards along the dotted lines. Add these to your word wall.

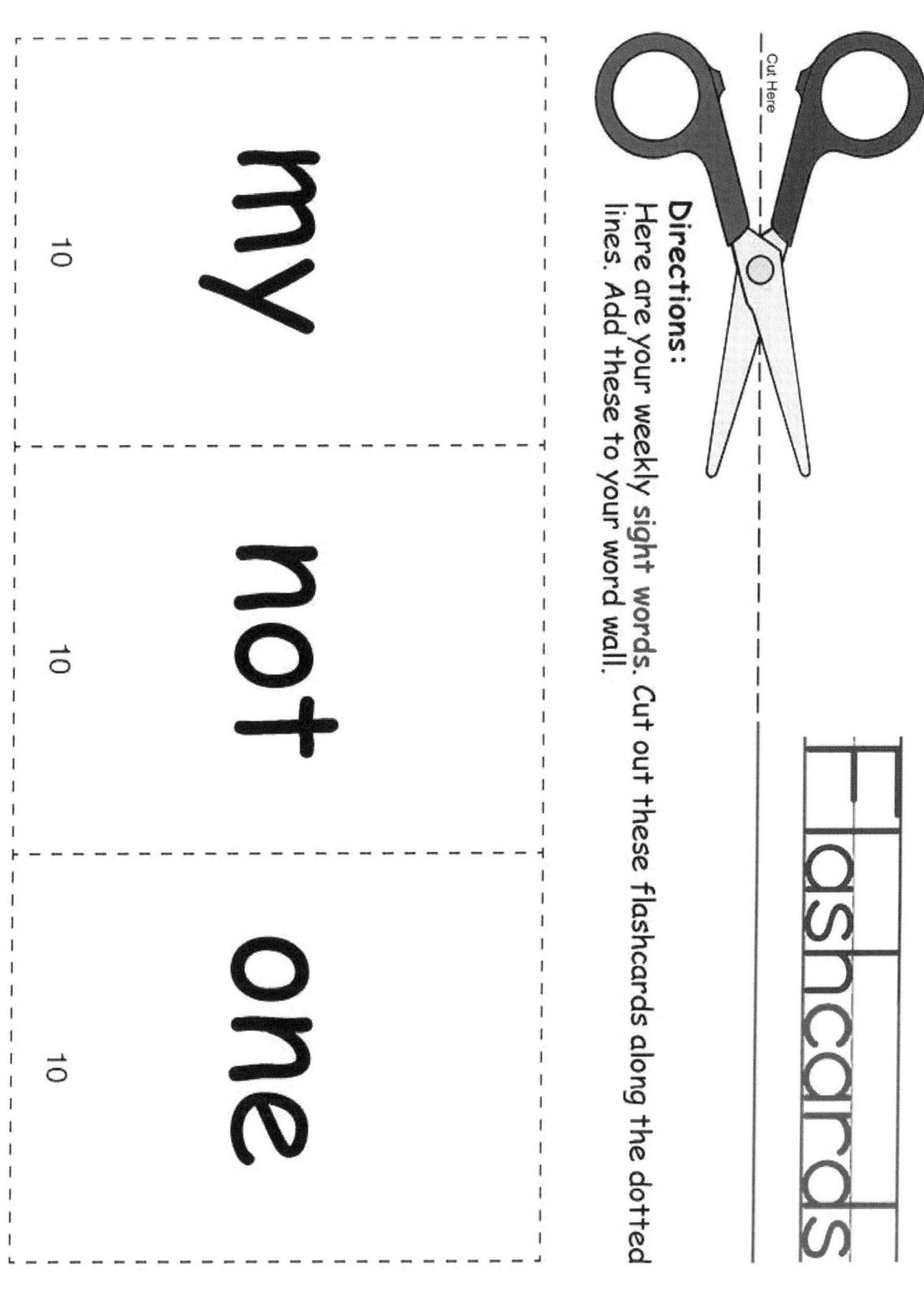

my	not	one
10	10	10

Directions:
Here are your weekly sight words. Cut out these flashcards along the dotted lines. Add these to your word wall.

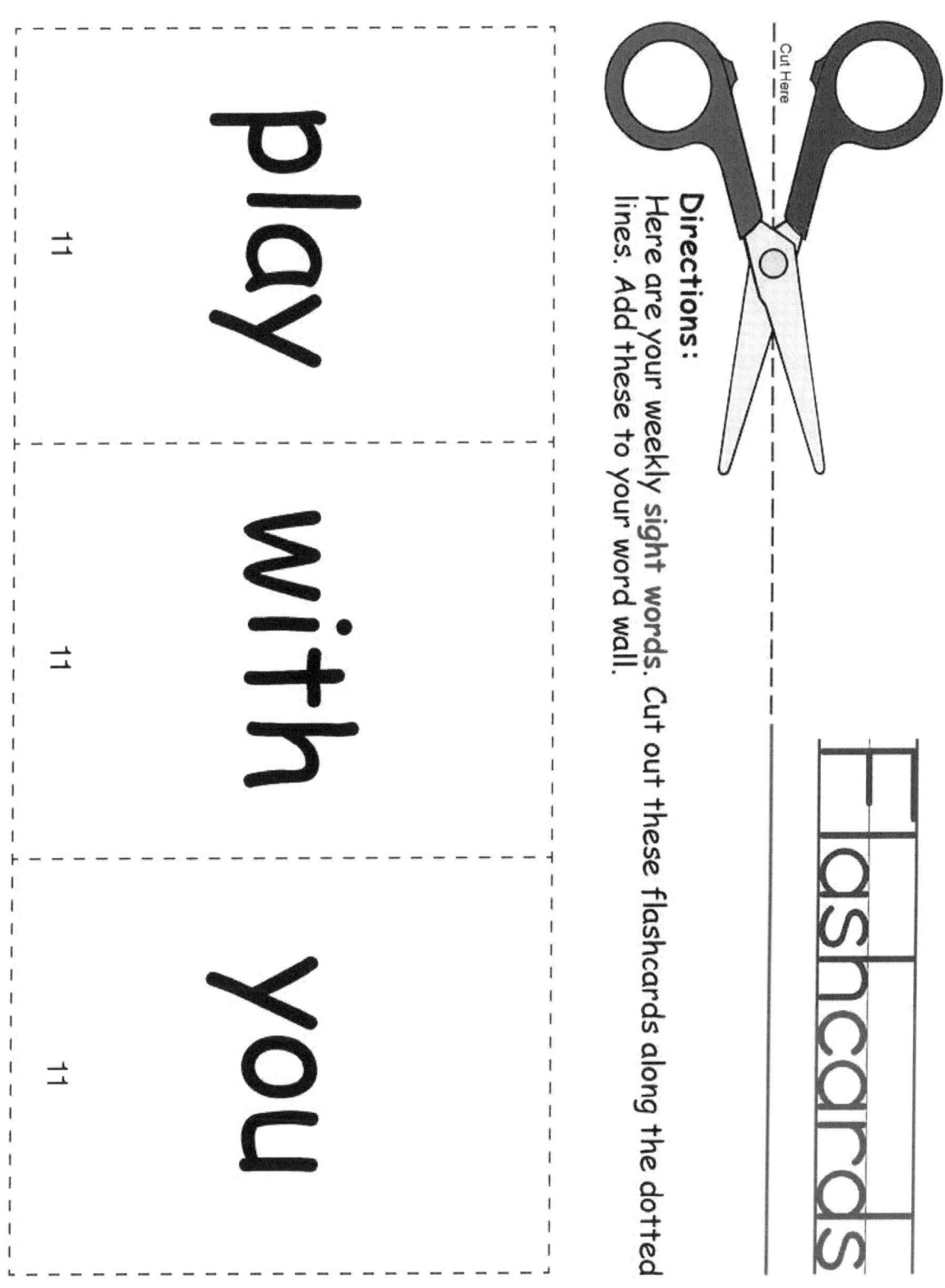

Flashcards

play	with	you
11	11	11

11.1 - Letter Ii

Sight Word Cards

Here are your sight words for this lesson. Cut out these flashcards along the dotted lines. Add these to your word wall.

Cut them out!

Flashcards

up 13

to 13

three 13

13.1 - Letter Cc

Directions:
Here are your weekly sight words. Cut out these flashcards along the dotted lines. Add these to your word wall.

Flashcards

| we | two | where |

14.1 - Letter Pp

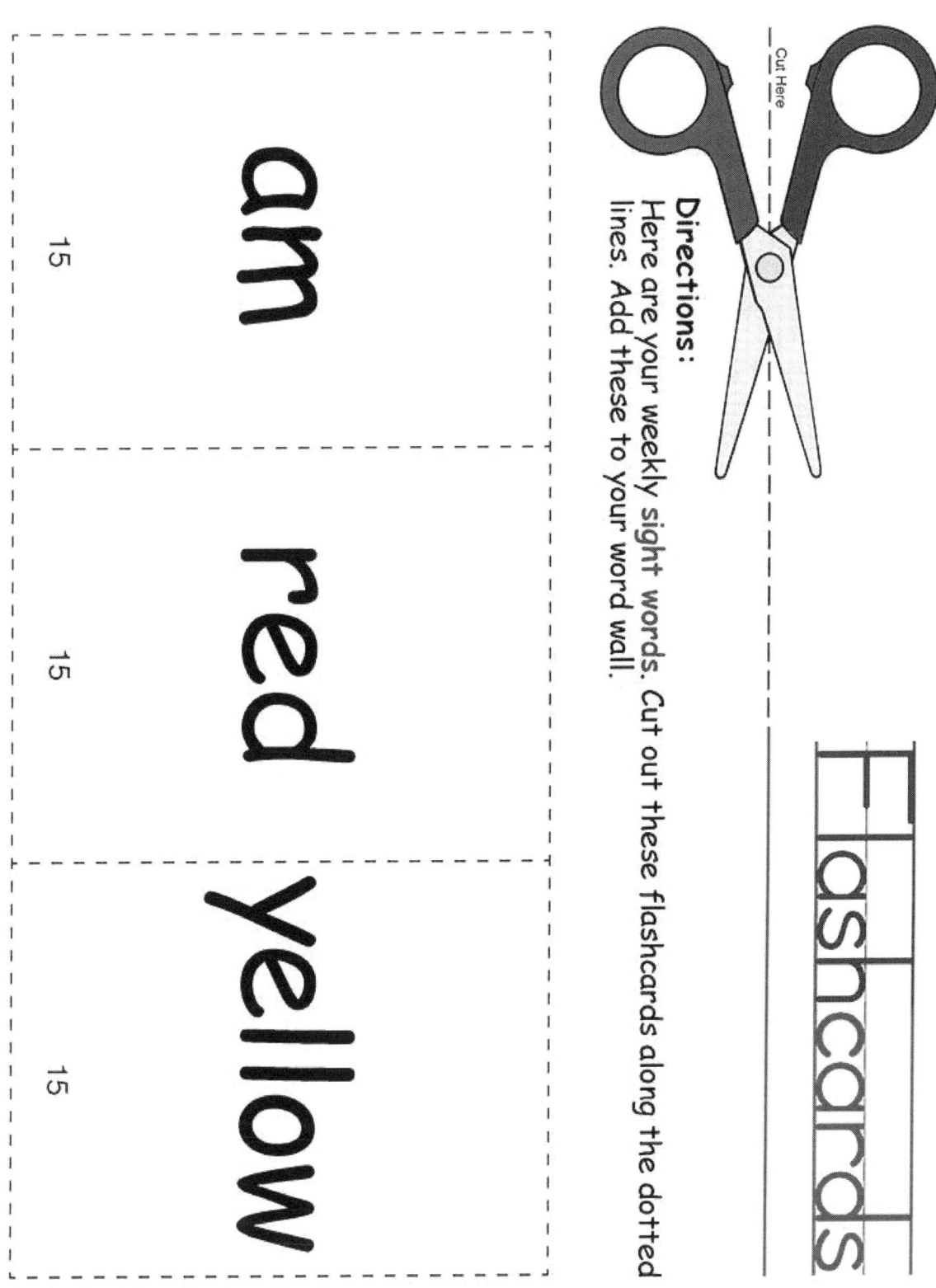

Directions:
Here are your weekly sight words. Cut out these flashcards along the dotted lines. Add these to your word wall.

Flashcards

am	red	yellow
15	15	15

15.1 - Letter Rr

Flashcards

Directions: Here are your weekly sight words. Cut out these flashcards along the dotted lines. Add these to your word wall.

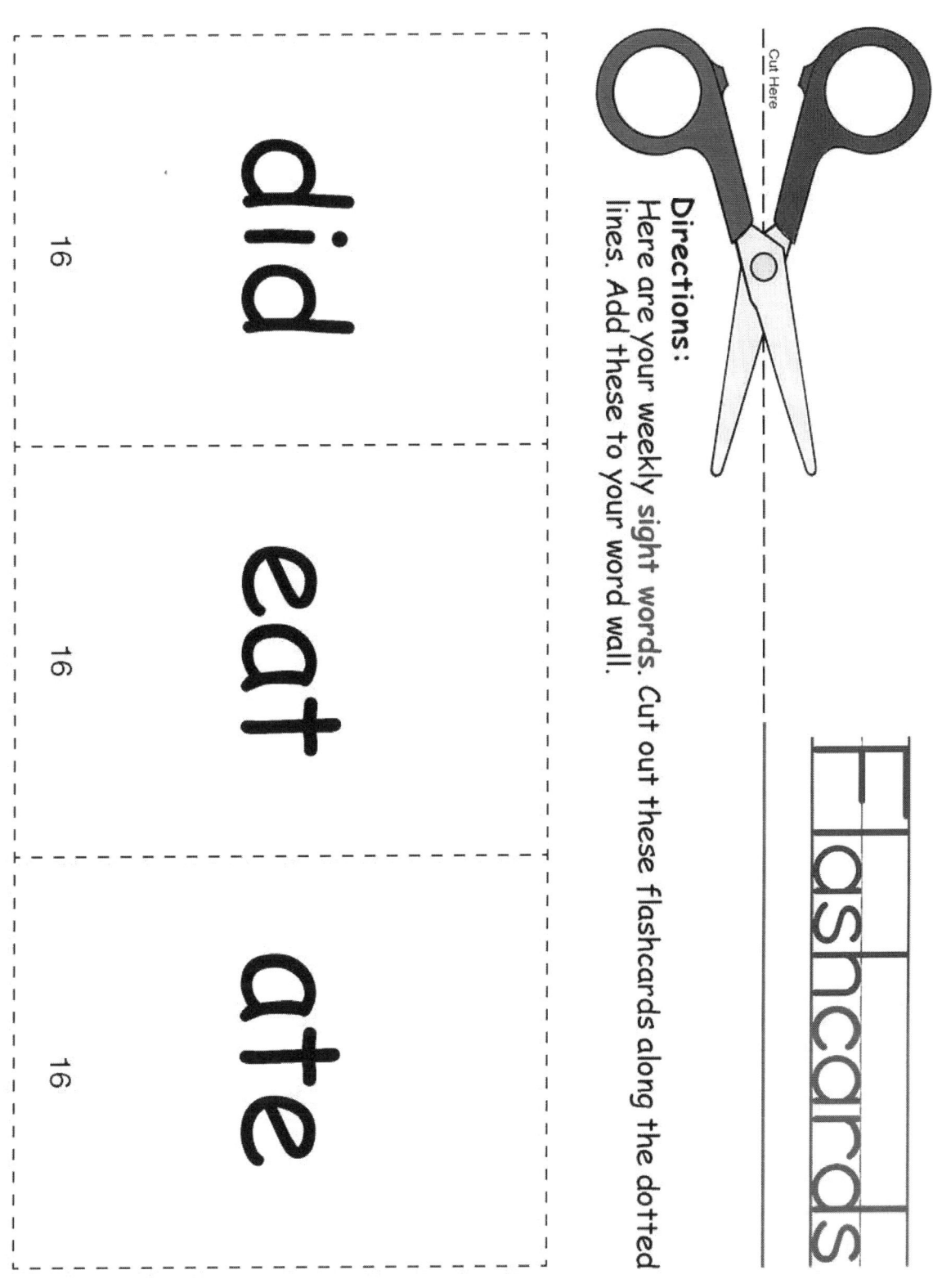

did	eat	ate
16	16	16

16.1 - Letter Oo

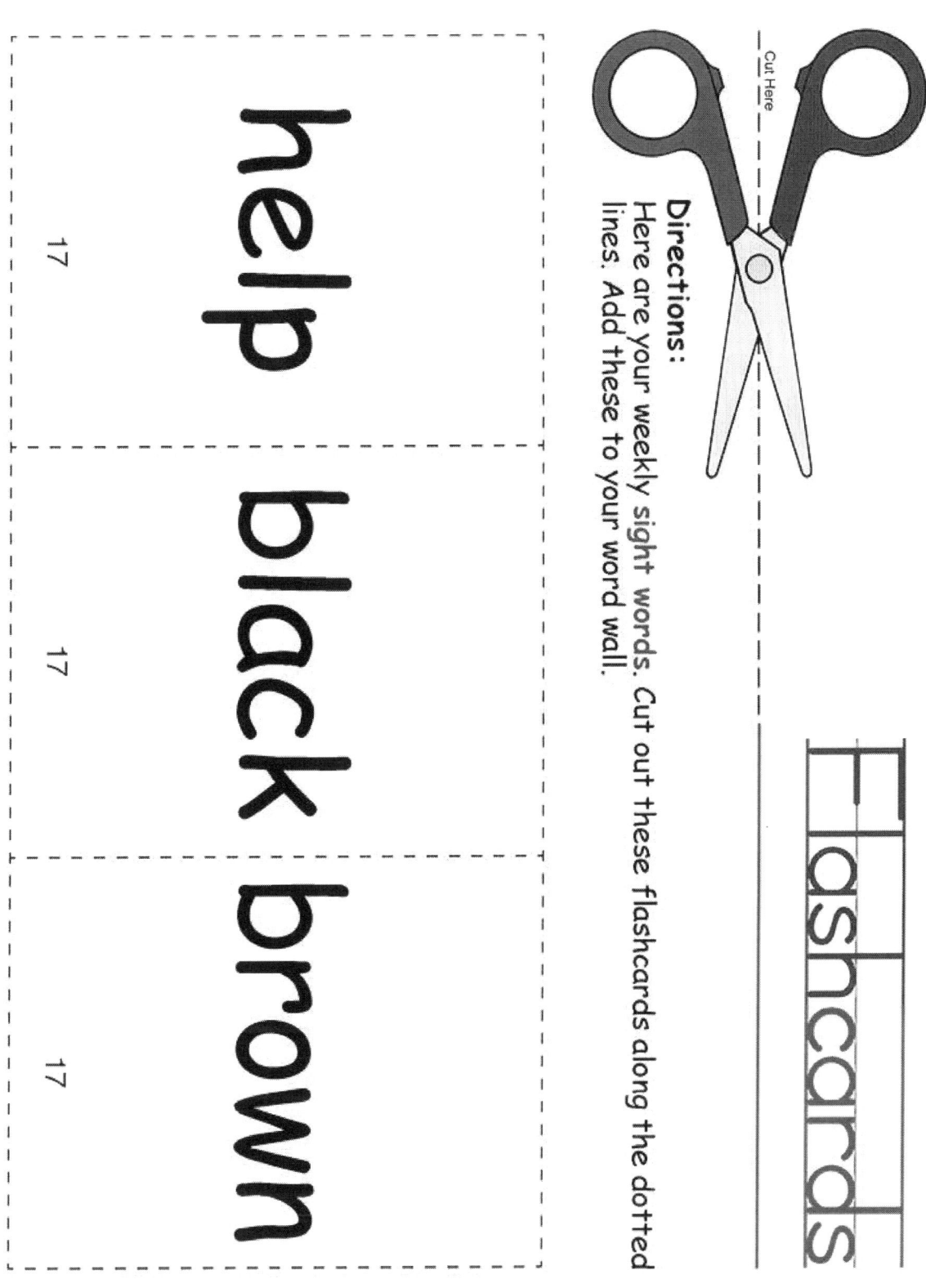

Directions:
Here are your weekly sight words. Cut out these flashcards along the dotted lines. Add these to your word wall.

Flashcards

help 17

black 17

brown 17

17.1 - Letter Hh